Sadie Shaw

Mosses from a Rolling Stone

Sadie Shaw

Mosses from a Rolling Stone

ISBN/EAN: 9783743343948

Manufactured in Europe, USA, Canada, Australia, Japa

Cover: Foto ©ninafisch / pixelio.de

Manufactured and distributed by brebook publishing software (www.brebook.com)

Sadie Shaw

Mosses from a Rolling Stone

Mosses From a Rolling Stone.

—BY—
SADIE SHAW.

CINCINNATI, O.
THE EDITOR PUBLISHING CO.,
1899.

Mosses from a Rolling Stone.

When anybody dreams a dream for five long years and then—it suddenly comes true, I wonder how anybody ought to feel?

Happy, of course! A little bit miserable too, and cross and tired with waiting so long for something that wasn't worth much after all.

Anyhow that's how I felt when my dream came true.

This dream wasn't such a very big affair, and I'd hardly dare tell you about it, if I didn't have faith in you and know you won't laugh in the wrong places.

Just to be all by myself in a big, far away city and see what I could do, anyhow! Away from the minister and his flock, and the circle of loving neighbors, and yes, even from all the relations unto the third and the fourth generation.

Never to slumber on parlor sofas anymore; never more to be tucked up in folding beds that are hidden away in dingy corners; never again to sleep "three in a bed," and then help do up the work next morning. Sweet, sweet dream!

And every night, when my other prayers were done I put in a P. S. to my own special little god, he who ruleth the Critics and the Editors, yes and even the two for a nickle magazine and the penny apiece.

I knew I wasn't worthy to do so much as loosen the latchet of his shoe so I prayed just for one small corner where I might "shine his boots" perchance, and so keep in touch with his godship.

And then—when it all came to pass, and I stood in that far away city surveying my little room with its *real* bed that was all my own— then would I have counted the whole world well lost just to be back home again and sit on the cellar steps and cry and cry and cry! I felt so dreadfully common-place. I slipped to the little mirror but it was not vanity saith the preacher, for I only wanted to see if I had the same old look I had worn for ages. Yes, and there were the freckles that spanned my nose—just the same—only there were eleven now and there used to be only ten.

I wondered why God had made me. I don't suppose I'm the first being who has wondered that in the light of his own reflection, only a pretty girl with sweet, dark eyes has no need to.

I can't help liking a pretty girl, and I'm not a man either! I don't care if she *is* flirtful and naughty and *does* wear silk-lined gowns, I can forgive her seven times seventy and a hundred fold, dear girl!

I guess if *you* were pretty 'twould turn your head too!

Once on a time when I was away at school I had a dainty sweet little room, so pretty that I used to go into the closet and peek out of it through the half-closed door. I never stood in the midst of it without a conscience stricken feeling that I was spoiling the effect. By and by I took unto myself a room mate, just as, sometimes, men take a helpmeet, because she was dainty and sweet and her blue eyes went so well with things and her fair hair matched the drapings. She whistled "Hot Time" from dewy morn till eve, and "Home Sweet Home" whenever I had the toothache, still I loved and cherished her and my greatest delight was posing her in the window seat and longing for the power to do her in water color. She was the model and I the artist—only, I couldn't draw a house so you could tell it from a chicken coop.

But I *do* like pretty things! Many, many moons ago, when I was fourteen, I fell in love with a—preacher. Not that *he* was pretty, oh no! but just wait till I get there.

Now, as I look down from the dizzy height of the years that have piled up since then I see myself as through a glass clearly, and behold! I was a very little girl, quite on a par with my china-headed doll with its sawdust heart, only we didn't know our hearts were sawdust then, that doll and I.

When I learned that this preacher had a wife I joined the band of martyrs and suffered and died for two weeks. The next week I figured as "Lucile." To be sure my hair was as tow and my eyes were pale, but I had a fertile imagination and 'twas but the work of a minute to have my hair all fall out and come in black as night. As for my eyes, I think I used diamond dye on them for they too "came in black." One day I met *her* and then—my love of the beautiful triumphed over my love of the preacher. Sorry—but I couldn't help it. Such a sweet, high-bred, dainty face as she did have; and "she was as good as she was beautiful."

That night I broke Lucile's head with my little hatchet. And if any man doubt me, let him remember his fourteenth year. Fourteen is the age of miracles, of all sorts of wonderful, marvelous things: one day we love John and the next we love Sue, and the day after we hate everybody and all his kin folks.

I would return to my subject if I only knew where it was.

"Lost, Strayed or Stolen: a subject! Anyone returning same to writer will receive a reward."

"Virtue hath its own reward."

"All's not gold that glitters."

"A thing of beauty is a joy forever."

There! I knew I'd find it in some old saw—it's *Beauty* my theme is. (I learned those old sayings at Normal School, glad now I went.)

Some big man has said that beauty

of mind is way above beauty of face. I expect he was an ugly animal.

That would be all right though if one could only wear the mind outside and get folk acquainted with it first, and then spring the face on 'em by degrees. If one could do *that*, why, we'd love each other better, old Socrates and I. You see, I beheld a picture of Socrates before I read any of his writings, and as I gazed on his brow and nose I readily understood how he could drink poison with a relish.

On a sunny afternoon long ago, I chanced to remember that, according to some man's tell, the eyes are the windows of the soul. I knew to a surety that I had a soul and I decided to have it peek out of its windows and get a glimpse of the great busy world. I had been reading some divine poetry and I felt so grand and great and good that I was sure my soul must be in its "Sunday best." I tip-toed to the glass. I gazed and gazed. Hush!

The windows were empty and I knew there were "Rooms to let!" I tiptoed back to my chair and in my heart was a feeling of goneness.

Bless the heart of the man who said beauty is in the beholder's eye. It's lucky for me if it *is* in the other fellow's eye, for now I won't have to "fix up" any more but just advertise for the right kind of an eye; one containing two beams and a mote with an eye winker in between. It must be color-blind and belong to a millionaire. Such an eye, I feel sure, can not fail to appreciate my style of beauty.

Gentle reader, when last seen in the body I was at the mirror counting freckles—away back there where I was wondering why I had been created.

I turned away from the little glass and there were tears dripping onto the bridge of freckles, but they couldn't wash it away for it was founded upon a bone and the winds came and the tears beat upon it but the freckles multiplied and grew strong.

Yes, I was weeping. Was this the girl who had prayed, not two weeks gone, "Oh, vision stay! Oh, dream turn real?" No! it was the other girl who claims she is a part of me, but you and I and Brown and Jones know better—*we* know she's a snide and an interloper. I took her up to the feet of Judge Reason.

"Why do you weep?" asked the judge. "Has not your dream turned real, your vision stayed? Are the ships on the Bay not as large as you dreamed, or the city, is it too small;— or have you ceased to aspire to 'blacking the boots' of your little god?"

The girl stamped her foot (and strange enough, but I did the same thing.) "What do you think I care for this trash? this! and this! and this! I want my dream—that's all."

Who says Reason has no heart? Not I! She had heart enough to leave that poor girl alone anyhow! And as for *me*, I had entirely lost my individuality in that of the "other girl" and which was t'other I didn't know. She had my entire sympathy, as I know she has yours.

You've all been there! Hugged a dream to your hearts day and night, longing with a fierce longing for it to come true—never realizing that it must die before it can be born—then all of a sudden you wake up with a little dead elephant on your hands and you wonder where your dream has fled. Folks point to the elephant and tell you that is your dream "turned real," but ah, you know better!

Did I say that or did some other fellow say it a long, long time before I was born? It makes me feel bad to think that no matter what I say it's all been said before. The only thing left for me to do is to turn it wrong side out, put on a new facing, hang it up on the line and beat it with a broom, till being already old and full of years, it falls to pieces and is then ready for the rag-bag. Ah's me!

But there I was, (I and the other girl, whom at last I had recognized as being one with myself) there I was weeping!

By and by my tears began to dry up and after mopping my face for an hour I struck dry land. I hailed it with joy, for I was hungry and needed my eyesight returned in order that I might seek food.

Reader, I was to do "light housekeeping" and there was a small back room for this purpose. This room was evidently intended to be lit by the star-light of my own eyes, for there were no apertures through which the rays of light might penetrate, excepting a transom and a key-hole. I entered this room.

"What a love of a place for developing pictures!" I said hoarsely. Then I cried in a loud voice, "Let there be light;" but the matches were not, and there was no light.

What I did in that room might have been "light house keeping," but if you had heard things drop from my hands, down, down into utter darkness, you wouldn't have called it so. I don't know what I partook of that evening, for only at rare intervals did I find the way to my mouth—and then, when I did, I gulped her down without regard to "race or color."

I said my prayers though. Somehow the darker it is the easier it is to find the place by your bedside to kneel. I remember just what I prayed: "Dear God, let me go right to sleep and forget all about everything and not wake up till ten o'clock."

And God did.

Which is another way of taking a Sedative.

The next morning I sat up in bed with a start. My window was open and I could hear the chirp and twitter of a little bird for it was springtime in the land. "But, surely, surely," I cried, "spring hath no word in all her vocabulary to describe the smell in my nostrils."

"Boiled onions!" whispered a little demon in my ear.

"That is the word," I muttered, "onions!"

The transom and the keyhole which proved such poor conductors of light did beautifully in conducting the rays of onions to my nose.

The morning waned, but the supply of onions did *not* wane. "Man does not live by onions alone," I cried, "can't that woman, if woman it be, cook anything else?"

It seemed she could, for presently the little demon whispered: "Cabbage, boiled dinner!"

After a time I crossed the hall to the store room, where my wood was piled. Reader, I knew that was my wood—anybody who stops to consider knows it too, yet when a wild-eyed woman came in upon me and announced that "that there wood, she'd have me know, belongs to the gen-'leman what owns this buildin'!" I dropped it and ran, and not until the "gen'leman" himself swore that he didn't own a stick of it, did I dare to touch it.

Even then I looked over my shoulder with fear and trembling, for I had a fearful presentiment that this avenging woman was the onion lady.

That same afternoon as I was passing an open door I heard someone singing such a sweet, cheery song that I stopped to catch a glimpse of the singer. Ah, I was pleased! Such a dear little woman, dainty and sweet and white-haired! I remembered old-fashioned pictures I'd seen, and when she smiled at me I thought of my mother. She beckoned me in. It was love at first sight, just as it always is with me. As I was leaving, she said: "I daresay you haven't done much cooking yet and I'm going to give you a little of mine." I made no protest—why should I? It pleased her to give, and it pleased me to receive, so what more does anyone want? She halved a pie and quartered a cake and then filled a china bowl with something, preserves no doubt—really, I thought, I must stop her.

Then I heard her saying:

"I almost know you're fond of onions—my husband and I like them so and I have to cook them fresh every morning so he can have them cold for lunch."

I murmured that maybe he'd want them.

"Oh no, I'll cook fresh ones in the morning," she said in her cheery way.

I carried them home to my room. I didn't touch the pie or the cake, but, reader, I ate every scrap in that onion bowl and licked my chops for more. 'Twould have been all the same to me if it had been a bowl of castor oil or of catnip tea for I wasn't feeding a dainty palate but a hungry, homesick, aching heart. I would have swallowed a whale if I thought it would please anyone.

The following morning when the little demon whispered in my ear I ordered him behind me, and I said, "God bless her! How good those onions do smell."

And my heart was lighter for having this reminder of her presence.

"Better a dinner of onions where love is," I muttered, and then laughed at my own folly, there being no one else to do it.

Not long after, a great lady came to call on me. She was the wife of the minister of the First Presbyterian Church in this city. She weighed, say three hundred pounds. I *do* hope her eyes were not the windows of her soul for if they were they must have been washed in butter milk and bluing. She sat down in my own little chair: I heard it squeak. So did she, and she asked if there were many mice in this "Institution."

Then the things which served her for eyes lighted on my books. "Oh, did I love to read? She just lived on reading—poetry was her specialty. Was I fond of poetry!"

In what contrary hour was I born that I, like Peter, should deny what I love? I looked her in her buttermilk eye and told her I couldn't abide it.

She was shocked. I was glad. Was it possible I didn't care for Browning or Shakespeare or Shelley or Keats or any of those lovely writers?

"Quite possible," I said, looking straight at those eyes.

"Of course," she said, "you don't care for Riley—"

Then the cock crew thrice and I bolted. When I returned I took the conversation by the horns and led it myself—Was she fond of onions? I asked. I just lived on 'em day and night, I said.

Then Mrs. Minister's eyes commenced to bulge and I could have knocked them off with a poker, only I feared spilling buttermilk on my carpet.

I then went on to tell her that if she'd sniff real hard she could probably smell onions cooking even now, as someone in this "Institution" was almost always fixing them.

She went. She thinks I'm crazy. I think so too.

When she had entirely disappeared I cried, and then went and got dear old "Riley" and kissed the brown covers and turned over the pages—not that I did not know every one by heart but I was just "taking stock." I felt as if someone had been trying to swipe my pet lambs.

Then I ran in where the Lady of the Onions dwelt and read her "Out to Old Aunt Mary's" in my best voice, and when I succeeded in bringing tears to her eyes I was happy, and Jim 'n me adopted her at once as one of "the relations."

But oh, it wasn't because the minister's wife was fat and had bluing eyes that I acted so mean! I wouldn't have cared how puffy her cheeks were if only her mouth hadn't been so little and hard and horrid; and somehow she made you feel cold and nasty and lonesome, and you almost knew she'd hold her skirts away from the dear old onion lady, and be "bored to death" if *she* ever went "Out to Old Aunt Mary's." She would weep at the reading of "Had a Hare-lip, Joney had," by the Reverend Mr. Minister, but if she ever met a real live Joney, in the flesh, sitting next her in church she'd roll out of the pew and pass by on the other side.

Well, may her bones rest in peace, if she's got any! Perhaps when she "shuffles off that mortal coil" she wears they will come to light.

There are thoughts that lie too deep for words and I guess that's what is the matter here. I want a word, a nice strong word that I can back up with an exclamation point.

I like exclamation points: I'd like to use one after every step I take. The word itself must be stirring and original—something to appeal to the hearts of my hearers and not a wicked, naughty word. It would be so easy if it were not for this stipulation; as it is, though, I've asked for too much. I'll use that mark anyhow! So there!

My room being in the tip-top story, its windows command a varied and interesting view.

The ships on the Bay, the mountains beyond; nearer, the Butcher's and Baker's and candle-stick Maker's and sundry back yards decorated from corner to corner with clothes-lines, all in full bloom. There are some women who wash six days in the week and on the seventh hang their bedding out to air.

I have been watching a little yellow dog in one of these back yards. I could see his small tail wagging and I knew by the wistful expression on his nose that he was hungry. I could tell by the turn of his tail and the cut of his hair that he was no aristocrat, but just a hungry, forsaken little street waif.

A woman appeared on the scene. She stooped to pick up a stone. She grunted—not that I heard her, but no woman of her size could help it. I looked at the stone in her hand; I looked at the little yellow dog; I winced. In my mind's eye I could see the wagging tail hung low between the shaggy legs. What matter if it wasn't the latest novelty in tails, nor his hair of a stylish cut, I couldn't bear to see the way he'd look back over his shoulder and whine. Then the woman lifted her arm; the dog yelped, and his tail disappeared in the manner I had foreseen.

For a moment I hated that woman with a fierce hatred, and yet, she had done a very natural thing. When things whine to us for what we cannot give: for sympathy or a bone when our hearts and our cupboards are both bare, why, we haul off and hit 'em. "A stone for bread," for so it is written.

When I came to myself I discovered a tear on my eyelid. "In the name of Sentimental Tommy," I said, "what are you crying about?"

"Nothin'," I answered.

"You aren't crying over a dirty little yellow dog are you?"

"Yes ma'am."

"Do you suppose for an instant that he's the only hungry dog in this city? Don't you know there are millions of 'em?"

"Yes ma'am."

And then all of a sudden this small dog became of Lilliputian size, and his suffering grew oh, so small and insignificant compared with what was daily borne by dogkind in general.

I had thought of stealing down the back stairway and buying some dog meat on the side, and patting his head and calling him "Gip" after my own little doggie that's dead.

But now I was discouraged—for what does *one* hungry dog, more or less, matter anyhow?

"Unto the least of these poor doggies"—whispered a still, small voice, and I slipped down the back stairway. I came home happy in knowing that one dog had had his fill that day.

The Lady of the Onions has been in for a chat. She has told me of a most incredible thing. She saw a young lady on the street, wearing rings on her thumbs! "A little off, perhaps," I suggested. But, no! She was very much "on," it appeared.

"She wore a beautiful dress," said the lady, "all trimmed inside and outside—mostly *inside*—with lovely pink silk, and she had to hold her skirt most wrong side out to get to show the trimming in it. But 'twas mighty pretty though! Still, it does seem like it would be handier to have things trimmed right side out." It did *seem* so.

"But why in the world did she put those pretty rings on her thumbs?"

she appealed to me once more. I ventured that perhaps they were too large for her fingers and this idea pleased her so well that she went away believing. As for myself, I knew in the innermost recess of my new tan shoe that I had fibbed monstrously. I feared, and yes, was almost certain, that this was but a new fad—this thumb business. Perhaps as yet it was only known to the cream of the "four hundred"—but how soon, ah how soon, would every little forsaken orphan be spending her last week's wages to purchase a brass ring to wear on her thumb!

"How long, oh Lord, how long," I cried, "before we'll have to wear rings on our big toes and go barefoot to show them?"

Speaking of the "four hundred" reminds me of my Aunt Cynthia. She was the dearest old lady, but a trifle back-woodsy—only I wouldn't advise anyone else to say as much. One day we passed a very elegant young lady on the street.

"Who's that?" asked Auntie. "Oh, one of the creams!" I answered indifferently.

"The what?"

"Belongs to the upper crust," I explained, but Auntie looked vacant.

"She's one of the 'four hundred'!" I said impatiently.

"I see," she said; "well it's a mercy, there's only four hundred of 'em; I guess we can hold our own yet awhile," was her placid comment.

Dear Aunt Cynthia! She never knew that it's "de quality" and not "de quantity" that makes this old world go round. Never knew that if "de quality" wear rings in their noses there isn't the ghost of a show but what "de quantity" must have their noses bored and be ringed at once.

But then it's nice being a "cream" and dressing sweet and even wearing rings on one's thumbs if it bring any pleasure. A woman's a woman for a' that, if—she don't lace! No woman can go on being a really, truly woman and lace at the same time. I know whereof I speak, for I've tried it. Just a teenty bit so's I could get my bran new gown together where it hooked under the arm. I bore it exactly one hour by the clock, and during that time I only breathed twice. I had grievous symptoms of apoplexy. My heart came up in my throat for air, and my thumb and forefinger sought my pulse! Heavens! I had no pulse! Yes, there it was, but how feeble! Then it stopped. My heart fluttered once in my throat; the table and book-case stood on their head; then all was still. I had ceased to breathe.

I bolted, and in two minutes time I was once again a live being and my heart was where it had first been placed. I will now quote from a great writer, who puts it rather strongly in these lines:

"Wear rings on your thumb-joints
And bells on your toes;
Your skirts wrong side out
And your hats on your nose;
Wear beads strung with nick-nacks
And powder your face;
But for love of your womanhood
Girls, do not lace!"

But not all the king's horses nor all the king's men can stop this unless writers of current literature cease having their heroines tall and slender, with waists so small that the hero can wind his arm twice around. Some day I shall write a novel—not now, not till I get this thing done—but some day. I'll take the exact measurement of my own immediate waist (all figures omitted here) and I'll have the heroine possessed of such a form. I know it will be a disappointment to many of my dear readers and to the hero himself, but I have bethought me of a sort of compromise. I shall have the hero's right arm twice its natural length. This may be painful to him at first, but I know my noble hero! I know he will cry out through set teeth that he is willing to bear this or any other pain if by so doing his own darling pet of a sweetheart will be enabled to breathe freely as God meant her to.

Won't it be soul-stirring? In the rooms adjoining mine is a new baby. It has such a "weary Willie" way of crying that I know it isn't onto its job yet. It takes a long time, much patience and strong lungs to learn to cry so it pays. A person who can't cry long and loudly is generally thought to be a failure, (oh, *did* Josh Billings say that?)

I'm rather sorry this baby came when it did, to be my little neighbor. It's a dear innocent love of a darling little baby-aby, I know, and I love it dearly in Song and Tradition, between book covers; but someway when the dear one cries in print it doesn't have that realistic touch as when only a veil intervenes betwixt us twain.

Babe, get printed! I know there is a large supply of accepted Mss. already on hand, but surely someone will print you, and then you can whoop her up bloody murder.

And yet, noise is healthy. I know it to be so. And it's the very spice of existence. I revel in thunder storms and a "Hot time" generally, up in the clouds. The cable car, the lumbering dray, the newsboy, all are dear to my heart. At night when the cable stops I waken at once and sleep returneth not unto me for an hour. A lumber wagon hath memories in every rumble, memories of a time when freckles were the delight of mine eye and the sun-bonnet remained on its peg in the hall, while I sat astride a yellow pumpkin, the very topmost one on the load, and the rumble of the wagon was music to my ear. Ah me! But there are noises and NOISES! This baby is the second kind.

One Sunday I hungered for rest

and silence. I found it at the end of a certain street car line, by a little lake in a grove of pines.

"In through the woods' green solitudes,
Fair as the Lord's Own Day!"

I murmured as I gazed, and a little bird sang like mad,—then silence; not so much as the dip of an oar on the lake. There was too much silence. I felt some as I do when the cable stops running. I fell to wondering if I'd enjoy living in Eden now. "Eden is out of date, a back number," I mused. "A body would miss the smoke and the buzzing and rushing and crushing," and then I forgot to think.

Rest, rest, rest! That was all I asked.

And the Pines kept singing in undertone: "In through the woods' green solitudes."

And a little bird trilled response: "Fair as the Lord's Own Day."

Eden is all right, it is *we* who are out of date.

I have composed a rhyme. I regret that I have not space wherein to print it, but owing to the large supply of Mss. on hand I shall be unable to do so. However, this does not reflect on the merit of the piece, etc., etc. No, I haven't room here for it. I simply wished to tell you that after composing it I found myself to be "The idle singer of an empty day." No, I err; "The *empty* singer of an idle day."

However, I'd rather be idle than empty. A rolling stone gathers no moss. I like moss and it's time I was gathering some. I've rolled about till it's all knocked off and my sides are sore for the want of it. When I'm dead and gone I wish to be always thought of as sitting by the roadside gathering moss. Heretofore I've been unable to do this. You remember I've lived with my relatives and slumbered on parlor sofas. Then too, I've sat under College Profs. from my youth. Not that I ever wore any moss off by study; I usually put one half hour of good study on my books and spent the remaining hours worrying because I hadn't studied longer.

Then I have kept a college Library! True, too true, the dust was many cubits deep on shelf and book, and there was madness in my method, still the grass wasn't allowed to grow under my feet nor the moss to gather on my back.

And what time, pray, have I had for collecting mosses during these latter days?

I've spent six weeks getting ready to go away to school; stayed one month by the clock, and spent six weeks getting ready to come back.

This beats the record of most rolling stones.

In those days I dreamed of a golden time when I might "lie at anchor" and gather moss "fore and aft" to use an expression whose purport I'm not exactly "up" on.

While I'm here I'll tell you what I know about marine matters. I know a ship when I see one, and a large body of water from a mill-pond. I know that a sailor and a Chinaman aren't necessarily one and the same being. I know if I ever went out in a boat all alone it would be just to feed the fishes, with no intention of ever coming home any more. I know if I ever got sea-sick on board I'd get off board and walk.

My brother has proved that water can be walked on, if stirred to the right consistency and placed in a refrigerator to cool. He has also proved that the earth is really flat after all, just as Columbus did—no, didn't—or did he? anyhow he did it or didn't it in 1942.

Babe is weeping again and I must retire to the bed and stuff my ears with pillow. To think that I must always fall asleep with my fingers jammed into my ear-sockets!

It must have been a dreadful thing to remain in the ark forty days and forty nights with nothing to read.

At that time Hawthorne was entirely unknown and Riley was not yet born. Of course, the Bible and Shakespeare and David Copperfield had been written, but very crudely, as typewriting was only in embryo then.

Dwelling on those olden days makes me turn with gladness to my own little book-case, filled with a "few well-chosen books."

I stop to call the roll:

"Pilgrim's Progress."—Absent.

"Has anyone seen Pilgrim's Progress lately?"

"No ma'am, not since you gave him to little Johnny Allen."

"Spurgeon's Sermons!"—Gone.
"Philosophy of Education!"—Lost.

(This is bad, very bad!)

"Riley!"—Here.
"House of Seven Gables!"—Present.
"Chestnuts!"—Here.
"Saintly Thoughts of a Little Girl!"— Dead. Etc, etc.

These books, absent company excepted are all dear to me—even the covers. Who was it laughed at an old gentleman who asked a book clerk for five middling sized blue books and five middling sized red books; and to be "pertikular about the readin' to have it plenty large?" Well, whoever laughed needn't have done it for size and color do make a difference.

I never feel content while reading Hawthorne unless I have in my hand a certain brown styled book just large enough to fit in the hollow of my hand. Hawthorne in any other garb is not quite Hawthorne to me. The mere sight of one of these books will carry me back a thousand miles and more than a thousand days, to a seat in a certain willow tree, where I perched for two days reading "House of Seven Gables." It was meat and drink to me, for I had been slowly starving to death on two hundred or more of Bertha M. Clay's, interspersed with Rosa N. Carey and Mary J. Holmes,—with E. P. Roe for dessert. How I ever passed safely through is more than I can say. I only know there was left a taste in my mouth such as might be produced by fifty cents worth of chocolate creams, three dishes strawberries—three slices nut cake and one floating island. My mind must have been wormy, I know; but when my mother suggested such a thing and intimated that my sweet disposition was spoiling on me I flew into a regular worm fit.

Hawthorne saved my life. At fifteen I entered the Poe age and "Ravens never flitting" and "Beautiful Annabelle Lee's," "Misty 'mid regions of Wier" and "Ghoul haunted regions of Wier," and all sorts of ghastly, ghostly haunted things went floating though my brain. In two months' time I had cast him aside and was wearing the covers off from "Lorna Doone" But the story itself never did grow threadbare and in spite of my destructive disposition it still holds for me the old time spell.

When I first read "Jane Eyre" I was just beginning to have "opinions" and "ideas" and I thought it befitting my place in life to air these as much as possible.

In the first place, Mr. Rochester wasn't a good man—even Jane acknowledged that. Neither need anyone think that his saying his prayers along at the last of the book was going to be enough, he'd have to say 'em every half hour for a year to make up for all *his* sins!

And why did Jane have to say she had green eyes? We need never have known it if she had kept still.

And it did seem as if Mr. Rochester might have gotten well in both his eyes while he was about it. He was ugly enough, goodness knows, with his hair and eyebrows and whiskers all singed off and his arms broke and his head bumped! And then to be blind as a bat—oh, dear!

Those were my sentiments at fifteen.

Now I read "Jane Eyre" as I do the Bible: a passage here and another there. When I feel religious I read it, and when I feel sad or poetical or sweet or happy or almost anything; sometimes for what *is* in it and sometimes for what *isn't* in it.

Oh, I'm not playing critic! I wouldn't dare to! But I'm just airing my feelings on this same. Though after all that is about all a critic can do: tells how *he* feels about it and makes believe it's you and I and Brown and Jones who feel that way. Instead of saying "*I think* this book is N. G." he asserts that without doubt "This book is N. G. and everybody with a grain of sense knows it!"

I wrote an essay on criticism once. I first mentioned the Critic. In referring again to said Critic I called him "he," the next time "she" and finally "it." I knew most critics were masculine and yet hadn't Mary Smith criticised my new hat shamefully, likening it to a war-ship?

And she was feminine. So to be *sure*, I used "it" just as men do when they can't remember to save their life whether the baby is "Mary" or "James."

My father used to say of me: "She's the sweetest little baby boy alive, so it is!"

I have been so lonesome this evening. I want to see my relations— even my wife's mother.

Speaking of relatives reminds me: I was once the beloved friend and confidante of five different relatives, all of whom hated the ground each other walked on. Each one thought I was just like herself. Mary would smile softly and say how like her I had become.

Jane said I was just her living image.

(Now Jane hated Mary and Mary hated Jane.)

Aunt Matilda thought I took after her more'n I did my own mother. I was like her, actions and all.

(Now Aunt Matilda couldn't abide Jane nor Mary, and vice versa with both Mary and Jane.)

Cousin Rhoda said I seemed to take the words right out of her mouth and say 'em 'fore she'd fairly done thinking them. "*We* must be a heap alike," she thought.

(Now Cousin Rhoda, Aunt Matilda, Mary and Jane hated each other, all vice versa and just like poison.)

Aunt Abigail, for whom I was named, said I ought to have been her child, for we were nearer alike'n two peas.

(Now Aunt Ab hated Aunt Matilda, Cousin Rhoda, Mary and Jane respectively and collectively, and they hated her in the same manner.)

I went through rich scenes: I suffered!

"How can this be," I cried, "if I am like Aunt Matilda, how then can Aunt Ab love me?"

"If I am the living image of Jane

how can Mary think me like herself and love me?"

"How can each one love one who is so like the other ones whom they each one of them hate, respectively, vice versa and like poison?"

Such things have driven men mad.

Yet it could be explained if only one could keep each one from the other ones who hated each the other and all the rest, respectively, collectively and like poison, excepting her own self and me.

Will no one help me?

It must be a beautiful thing to have command of the English language. I do wish something could be invented so one would only have to think his thoughts in a nice little machine and have them come out in good, plain, old-fashioned English.

Oh, to get this relative business straight before I die!

But I wander. I was lonesome, didn't I say? Well, whether I said so or not, I was, and I longed for anyone of those relatives alone, without any of the others who each—there I go! Help! Murder!!

Let's change the subject. It needs a change: everything does. I need it, need it bad! If I had change I wouldn't be lonesome but would be planning what to buy to-morrow. I did have a little change this morning but it took it all for postage stamps for the letters I wrote to Mary and Ja—(I mean kindred. Here let me say that never again in my presence do I wish those names mentioned. The word "kindred" will convey your meaning without giving details or calling names.)

It's wrong to call names. I have been called names all my life long. If ever I meet the man who first called me "queer," there'll be trouble.

It has clung to me always; no matter how hard I've tried to live it down and be just like other folks, still people have wagged their heads and cried among themselves, saying:

"Did we not hear it said this person was accounted 'queer,' by many?"

It is interesting to note how many different words are used to denote one and the same quality. There are certain words that appeal to certain classes of people: If my enemies galore wish to describe me, they call me "queer;" my semi-enemies remark indifferently that I'm rather an "odd body;" those who feel kindly toward me but yet do not know my real worth, say I am a little "eccentric." My own mother and two others have said that I'm a truly "lovable, sweet, unusual" girl.

This use of words as given above, is called wordogogy, meaning, the Science of Words.

For five long days now I have heard a voice singing anthems to the new baby in the next rooms. First, I thought it was the mother, but since then I've learned that it's a young auntie who works in a telephone office.

I hadn't supposed this possible of a telephone girl. Many long years have I listened to her sweet voice through the 'phone, calling: "Number, please?"

And again: "Line's busy, call again!"

And once again: "Pike 1-4-2 will not reply!"

I have listened to this until I had learned to love her dear tones; but now, day after day she rends my heart asunder and I cry: "Babe, howl louder!" and baby does.

One should keep one's place in this world. Because this young woman's voice soundeth sweet through a 'phone is no reason for her setting herself up as a baby prima-donna.

I love music, though! I have a cousin who sings songs without words, while I sing words without song—I sing them through my nose in my elocution class, Mondays and Wednesdays. Tuition free! I know a dear lady who sent her only daughter away to get voice culture.

Well, and she got it!

But when she returned we girls had ourselves vaccinated for fear we might catch it. Hers was a severe case and her throat is not real strong and well yet. I always have been afraid of throat diseases.

But there *is* music in the world, and sweet singing. I heard the sweetest I shall ever hear a long time ago.—Sometimes I hear it yet, in dreams, when I have fallen asleep, weary—with my face all wet with tears. It is the same voice I used to hear when I had the earache and mother rocked me to sleep; and those are the same songs she used to sing too; one was about a poor little boy who was blind, and it had twenty verses. I know *now* how mother's throat must have ached, but *then* I only knew that the ache in my ear grew fainter and fainter and by the time the twentieth verse was done—I was asleep.

Voice culture is a lovely thing, and when I'm strong and well I love to hear the singing of earth's great ones, but oh, when I have the earache then let mother sing to me:

"That little boy was blind."

It is the dinner hour. I hear footsteps approaching. I know their gender is masculine and their boots are 16x24. The waves of sound smiting upon my eardrum tell me this. Some women claim they can tell when their husbands are returning by their steps on the walk. Of course they can if they go about it right. All they have to do is to find the exact size of husband's foot. Then ascertain how large a dent on the ear-drum has been made by sound waves produced by said foot hitting the sidewalk. Then when a step is heard on the walk just measure the dent made on the eardrum and if it corresponds to the dent caused by said husband's foot, why, it's him. (Only be quick about it or he'll get in 'fore you get it done.)

If there is any student who doesn't understand this I refer him to Dr.— whom I sat under in Physics in '72. When I used to keep the college library I could clearly distinguish the president's step from those of professors or students. Not by the above approved method, but by one quite as satisfactory. He always came down the long hall on tip-toe; stood at the door for five minutes to discover if there was hilarity within and then burst in like a shot! This manner of his coming gave me plenty of time to hide all traces of the rhyme I'd been making about his chin; to hush the students and resurrect the book of classification which I sat on during his absence. Only once did he surprise me, and that was when he came down the hall walking after the manner of man: Then was I undone!

This president was a good man,

the beloved of his flock, but our natures were strangely at variance. He looked upon me as librarian, one who was drawing a small stipend and was expected to work a little for it. I couldn't see it in that light; heretofore, from my observation of librarians as a class I had come to the conclusion that a librarian is a very fortunate person, one who has a snap and has struck it rich all 'round. I thought her sole duty was to sit with her feet on a stool and read the books committed to her charge. She was paid, I supposed, because she was a special favorite of the board of trustees. This is what induced me to apply for the job.

But when the president gradually instilled into my mind the fact that things were not to be thusly, I resigned. I couldn't do otherwise, entertaining as I did these sentiments of freedom, liberty and equality.

But that was long ago. Now as I review that olden time my only wonder is that I didn't get my neck wrung like a chicken. If asked what I consider man's strongest traits of character, I should reply: "Patience, kindness and all charity: Librarians a specialty."

The windows of my room do not embrace a view of the whole bay, and though I do not see it, yet, I know of a certainty that a steamboat approacheth. I know it—not by its foot-step—but by its voice. It has a strong full voice but I'm afraid it has caught "culture." It begins low like the moan of one who has a tooth-ache; then it rises till it reaches the howl of those who cry in torment; higher up the scale it touches the key of all human misery, and then follows a prolonged note and in vision I see a pair of forceps grasping an ulcerated tooth. Behind all these strains of music is a little gurgling note of satanic glee, and in vision again I behold the dentist, who with dancing eye wields the forceps and gloats over the length of that bloody tooth.

My nerves are raw and bleeding; my ear drum punctured! My brain throbs! Oh, if one could only be forewarned of this, but no man knoweth the hour of its coming. The time card says at such and such a time will the "Flyer" enter her dock. At the stated time I place my ears beneath the pillows and leave them there for what seems an hour, then I remove them and sit down as is my wont. At that instant the voice of the Flyer is heard in the land.

"Hark! hark! the dogs do bark!
  The beggars are coming to town.
Some in rags and some in tags
  And some in a velvet gown."
Old Ballad.

One moment I see a frayed skirt and the ragged fringe of a shawl fluttering in the wind. The next, an Easter hat and a silk lined gown.

But they're all beggars just the same. I'm glad of that—glad the ones in the velvet gowns have to beg for happiness exactly as often as the ones in the ragged shawls.

True, they knock at different doors: "Please ma'am, might I get a little something to eat? I'd be willing to work for it," says the waif at the door of a rich lady.

"Please ma'am, might I come to your parties and teas? I'd be willing to work for it," says the rich lady to society's ring-leader.

"Please might I have a moment of rest and peace and contentment? I'd be willing to work for it!" and Society's leader knocks at the door of her own closed heart.

Often as not the door goes shut with a bang and the bolt is made fast.

But here is life in a nut-shell:

If you're hungry, work!

If you can't get work, beg!

If you can't beg, steal!

This is human nature and this is why I must steal—into my little dark room and do dark housekeeping. I hate to, I wasn't brought up to it, but "Oh, I am hungry!" said little Tim or Tommy or Johnny or somebody with a name mentioned in my elocution book.

After all, what's in a name! A little boy is just as hungry, whether his name is Tim or Tommy or Abigail, which is mine, you remember, I being named after my aunt.

What's in a name? Would not the works of Riley be just as sweet by any other name? No! a thousand times, No! Do you suppose I'd ever have read a one of them if they'd been called "The Book of Ezra," or of "Nehemiah," or "Obediah," or of "Amos?" Never!

What's in a name? Why, if Bill Nye had signed his name to "Saintly Thoughts of a Little Girl" you'd have to laugh in spite of yourself. And if I should write a poem and sign Kipling's name I'd be famous at once—but Kipling wouldn't, not so much so—nit!

Maybe a rose *is* just as sweet by

any other name, but I'll bet if you'd tell your sweetheart you were going to send her a box of "cabbages," (meaning roses) I'll bet you'd get the G. B. at once.

G. B., gentle reader, means "good bye." It doesn't mean that to a college bred boy, but to his papa and mamma that's what it signifies. When he writes home and says the president has given him the G. B., they of course believe that the president has gone away, tenderly saying "good bye" to their darling son.

"To him that hath shall be given."

To him that hath 10 cents shall be given a place to spend it.

To him that hath a wife shall be given a mother-in-law.

To him that hath 11 offsprings shall be given one more to make it 12.

"To him that hath not shall be taken away even that which he hath."

I know this to be true. To him that hath not the wherewithal to pay his rent shall be taken away even the room which he hath, by the "gen'leman that owns the buildin'."

The tramp knows it to be true. To him that hath not any shirt shall be taken away even the one which he hath, swiped from a lady's clothes line. For this is the law of the Medes and Persians, of the United States and Great Britain.

I've never yet mentioned what country I dwell in. I own several castles in Spain; two on the Rhine near Fair Bingen, and one estate in England. But if you want to find me to home just call at this building an' the gen'leman what owns it will show you up. The elevator isn't running now but there are only four flights of stairs to climb, and going down you can "drop a nickle in the slot," mount the banisters and *slide*. Be careful not to knock the knob off the banister at the bottom.

"And the moon shines bright on the Wabash," shrieks the broken organ, grinding in the street below. There are no words too strong to use in deridement of the organ grinder, and yet, I, being rather "queer" and "odd, to be sure," revel in this thing. The old Romans, you remember, when in trouble, delighted to hear the groans of their slaves; it eased their own fierce pain to know that someone else was suffering worse than themselves.

That's me, precisely, exactly, hitting the nail right side up! As I listen to the piteous organ grinder I know that there are depths of misery such as I have never sounded, and the louder he groans and the wilder he grinds the more contented I feel. However, I'm not entirely without mercy and when I think he's suffered enough I go down and give him a dime, and then come home, puffed up, patting myself on the back and hoping some good minister around the corner saw me do it. I shed a few frog tears and am then at peace with myself and all the world.

"Bless the organ grinder!" "And the moon shines bright on the Wabash."

I would rather rock all day long than to write a Dictionary. Rocking is my vocation.

I am the only one of my family who takes after me in this excepting my little niece, who is said to be like me in more ways than one. You bet I love her too!

Whenever she tears her apron from hem to neck band she is then said to be like her Aunt Abbie. If perchance, she cuts papers all over the carpet and then refuses to pick them up and gets sassy—she is again like her auntie. When she screams and kicks at table for two cups of coffee strong enough to float a turkey egg, she, of course, takes after auntie.

Only when she's a good little girl and says her prayers then she's like papa and mamma and Uncle Moses.

Maybe they don't know that auntie is good and says her prayers too sometimes. My little niece isn't named for me, of which I'm glad, for whatever there may or may not be in most names, in mine there are seven of the ugliest letters in the alphabet. It isn't an inspiring name. *Inspiration* is a peculiar thing. It is generally thought to be the quintessence of spirituality, but like most quintessences it comes done up in very earthy packages. I rise in the morning; I gaze out of the windows; I say : why should I make one effort to-day, why perspire and hurry; what will it all matter one thousand years from date; why need my eyes open more than is necessary or my feet move restlessly to and fro? I will eat a bite of breakfast not because I'm hungry but because all men must eat as well as die.

I prepare the coffee; I take two sips and begin to prick up my ears; four sips, my eyes pop open; one half cup; if this day should pass without my having tipped up a corner of the universe then would I be undone! One and one half cup, all things are possible to me, I could remove mountains if I had the time, but I have no time—I must hasten; two cups, my nerves are being wound up by an invisible hand—they are taut now and my knees spring up when I walk just as they did when I used to wear my elastics too tight; Life is a great thing. There is much to do and I alone am left to do it. Let me hasten! There is inspiration in a coffee cup. Mind though, and don't buy imitation coffee mixed with chickoree, found at all dealers.

With coffee I generally eat a roll and a doughnut. At first I used to save the doughnut for dessert, eating the roll as first course, but I soon saw my mistake. The sugar and shortening had all gotten into the roll, and what had gotten into the doughnut I never knew. It was called a "raised doughnut" but not all the king's horses nor all the king's cows could ever have raised it an inch. It should be cut in thin slices, buttered and eaten slowly. Think on solemn things and never indulge in hilarity, for if it ever gets into your windpipe, you're a deader. When once eaten it sinks, settling somewhere in the toe of your shoe. I'm always scairt to death for fear it'll lodge in that little pocket that catches grape seeds and eggshells and things.

Another night and another morn, and behold, it is another day! Last evening I was enticed away to an entertainment which ended in an old-fashioned dance, "old as the hills," to the on-looker, but a "new blue" to the dancer. Don't deceive yourself by thinking I was merely an on-looker, neither was I a "wall-flower," for I sat as far from the wall as possible and so near to the dancers that a lady with an immense big sash caught her skirt binding, in one of its weakest places, on the toe of my shoe—there was a corn on that toe, too!

As for my looking on, why, I danced every set, not with my feet, but with heart and eyes. I completely lost my individuality in the crowd. I was here and there and everywhere. Now I was that pretty girl with a face like a flower, making sweet eyes at her partner and flushing whenever she met his hand in the rollicking dance. Now, that dark eyed woman who was coquetting with her husband just as though they hadn't been married for forty years or more. Now, that jolly fellow who had such ado to keep from flying all to pieces. He swung his partner as if he were winning a battle, and the perspiration rolled down his face and mine too, 'twas such jolly hard work. And when the "greenies" got lost, as "greenies" will, why, there I was in the ring, laughing for all there was in it; and once, I was one of the greenies myself, blushing and feeling awkward but happy through it all.

And then—ah, somebody has awakened me by punching an elbow through my rib. It was one of the wall flowers, so I perforce turned my attention to them. Many of them were quite pretty.

"Do you never dance?" asked a young lady who had been on the floor every set.

"No, indeed!" replied the wallflower, "Mama doesn't like me to."

Another said, "Papa didn't believe in it."

Another didn't "care for it." And yet another "never had learned and never intended to, and what was more, she wouldn't learn for anything."

They were all looking sad and miserable.

Dear girls! they were happy enough looking on only they were so afraid someone would think them miserable that they *were* miserable. So afraid the dancers would pity them! Why, I'd like to see them pitying me; they'd be pitying one of their own gang if they did!

And here let me say to all ye merrymakers, ye who dance and ye who sing and play on stringed instruments, "Never pity anyone because they are not one of you, for often and often their hearts are beating in time with every tap of your foot on the floor."

Pity is getting threadbare—it's a poor thing now days.

There was once a young lady. She and I pitied one another greatly. She pitied me because my skirts hung so abominably; I pitied her because hers didn't, because her hair was dressed to a nicety and her hat a dream; because every detail of her costume was perfection itself. I pitied her, I say, believing as I did that no one could devote her time to such things and have any room left for higher thoughts. I called her "The Body," and looked upon her as a mere dress form.

One day we met on a point overlooking the Bay. I had been sitting there alone, thinking "high thoughts" and glorifying nature, also congratulating myself that I was not as some others. Then something came between me and the sun. It was The Body.

Bitterness came into my heart. What right had she in such a place? Her sphere was at the milliner's or the hair dresser's. She desecrated this place and shut out the light. My mouth tasted of wormwood and I was conscious to my finger tips that my hair was a thing of wildness and a grief forever; that my shoes had all the tan worn off and my skirt was out of plumb. And there she stood— The Body!

Suddenly she turned and faced me. Was that The Body?

Her eyes were full of tears and her face was quivering strangely. Then I heard her saying:

"Isn't it sweet and quiet here, and don't the mountains over yonder make you homesick? I live in dear old Montana," she added.

Then our souls were knit together, and I sidled up to her and we looked out at the blue Bay and the world of mountains beyond. I saw clearer and farther than ever before, for I looked through four eyes *now*, and two of them were sweet and dark.

Do dark eyes see better, or is it only because I am so dead tired of green?

"A Yard of Roses," "A Yard of Pansies," or "A Yard of Puppies?" You all have them—everybody has—and they're framed and hanging over the door where "Home Sweet Home," done on card-board used to hang.

For myself, I have "A Yard of Dandelions." It has no frame excepting an old rickety three-rail fence, and it hangs right across the street. It isn't one of those *back*-yards I've mentioned either, but is all by itself, void of house or chicken-coop. It's one of the few places in this world of utilization that has gone to waste and filled up with such rubbish as wild currant bushes and big yellow dandelions. But I'm a wasteful being by nature, and so I glory in it, and so does a little bird I know who spends half his time singing "Glorias" to the sun and dandelions.

Oh, if I only could lie down and tumble and roll in that green grass and pick my apron full of those wild flowers, and sing and laugh and holler like a free born thing!

Well, why not, there's no law against it.

No! no law excepting a little bitter mocking one, not written but whispered and thought and spoken: "What would people think?" bears. as much weight as any legalized statement in Blackstone.

But be independent! What is it to you what people think? If you want to sing and holler in a bed of dandelions what matters it what anyone says?

Well then, I'm cornered, and the question is, "What would I, my very own self think, I who am old and full of years; would not my bones wax old at my rising up and my sitting down; would not my knees knock together when I jumped? And lo, when I hollered how strange my voice would sound to my own ears!

No, I cannot, cannot do it! Would that I were that curlyheaded child of long ago who sat astride the yellow pumpkin and rode through her little world in state; who bored her brown toes in the mud and stored up sunshine and freckles, scratches and blisters, daisies and dandelions all in a moment and for all time to come.

Still, that child, happy in her play, was as one who is happy in slumber, entirely unconscious of the great, good thing that was hers; she was happy but knew it not. So I wouldn't be that little girl after all, for when I'm happy I want to know it and be able to crow over it and philosophize about it. I hate to go to sleep at night, I want to stay awake and enjoy and appreciate the grand sleep I'm having.

So here I am back at the old place and all I can do is to enjoy my dandelions at a distance, and wish my little niece were here, then I'd have her do the singing and tumbling—have her take the happy part, and I'd stand by to tell her exactly how happy she ought to be and what a great, grand privilege was hers—whereat, she, thinking I was reproving her or scolding her, would set up a howl and cry bloody murder and then—I'd have to spank her—and oh dear, that yard of dandelions is more trouble to me than an acre of puppies would be!

I'll not look at it any more. I'll look far, far away, where I see a big white pile of clouds—no, it's a mountain—it's Mt. Rainier! I used to see this mountain a long time ago in my geography, but it didn't look as it does now. It has changed wonderfully. *Then* it was only a few little black marks whose name I couldn't remember. The fact that it was 14,444 feet in height was of minor importance to me, and when asked for the figures I always replied, "44,414 feet, ma'am."

But it's changed since then. It is a great white mystery, and as I behold it, now, melting into the clouds; now rising out clear against the blue sky with only its white crown in the mist, then am I minded of the Book of Revelations and of what John saw and heard; and if I had seven candlesticks with seven candles in them I'd light them at once as sort of a religious rite. I love this old mountain so much more than I did when it was only a few black scratches in my geography.

Geography never appealed to any of my emotions excepting to one of pity for myself when I realized how small my brain must be since I couldn't remember for twenty-four hours which dot was which and what it was named. I'd hate to be asked to-day where the Bay of Biscay is. I know I should love it if I ever saw it in the flesh, a real live body of water and not a little squab of green on a musty old page. I'd love to sit by it all day long; to row on it and to dream by it—but don't expect me to know where it is.

I tell you I don't know where anything is. I don't know where my hat pin is this very minute, nor my handkerchief nor my lead-pencil nor my gloves nor anything that is mine.

I don't know where my subject is. I lost it long ago. My dandelions have shut up shop for the night so I can't find them either. They're lost somewhere among the grasses and currant bushes.

Things have come to a pretty pass, though, when you can lose a mountain like old Rainier, yet this have I done. It's somewhere, somewhere among the mists and the clouds—but where! I've looked till my eyes ache, but I can't find my mountain, nor my hat pin, nor anything that's mine, and I'm mighty tired.

A dew-drop face in a frill of lace,
A streamer of ribbon blue;
A vision bright in a gleam of light,
My sweetheart, that is *you*.

A whiff of rose and there she goes
Like a rainbow through the Blue.
She cannot hide for the world is dyed
With the radiance of her hue:
My sweet-heart, that is *you*.

After writing the above I felt so sorry to think no one ever writes poems to men sweethearts. Hasn't any one got a sweetheart who isn't a woman? Or is man such an ugly animal he can't be rhymed about in poems to sweethearts? I think not. It ought to be done and I'm the one to do it, so here goes:

A sun-flower face in the sweet embrace
Of a collar built for two:
A nose that's broke in a stream of smoke;
My sweet-heart that is *you*.

A whiff of pipe and he goes like
A shot gun fired by Dew—;
He cannot hide for his necktie's dyed
To a shade that's rather—too!
My sweetheart, that is *you*.

I feel so much better. But there are some men who never are anybody's sweethearts. They never have anyone to love them or dry their tears or wash their pocket kerchiefs; nobody to sew up their jumpers or put buttons on their overalls; nobody to warm their cowhides when they are all damp with the dews of the irrigating ditch and soiled with clay from the highway. This lone man trudges home at night, but nobody lights his pipe for him as he sits by the fire and steams; nobody runs up and kisses his tousled moustache and talks to him with a sweet caress in her voice. True he has had a wife— had her for twenty years—he has her yet! But he isn't her sweetheart. He used to be long ago, before the war—no, I err—it was *she* who was the sweetheart, his "little sweetheart," and she is still, but *he* is just "Bill, her man."

Maybe he's dead now, dear old fellow! and his wife is living on the insurance money. Of course she calls him "her Willie" now, and wipes her froggy eyes on a black bordered handkerchief which she keeps in a black pocket which is sewed into a black apron which covers a black dress worn by a black woman with a black heart. May her bones rest in black!

As a rule relatives-in-law aren't loved. I never had a mother-in-law so I can't say as to that, but I dote on sisters-in-law. I have some eight or nine of them and I think this qualifies me to express my opinion.

They are most of them younger than I, only one may be a month or so older and another six weeks—but they are *mostly* younger, yet they all mother me and call me "little Abbie;" and though I stand head and shoulders above them they take me under their wings and love me and show me how to darn my stockings and sew on my buttons. They seem to know by instinct how frail my knowledge is, for if I, perchance, offer to help them a look of trouble creeps into their sweet eyes and they say: "Not now, darling. Run out and play—see," they cry, "see the pretty sunshine!" So with glee in her heart and an infantile smile "little Abbie" runs out to play—for "little Abbie" loves to play.

Sometimes I sidle into the kitchen and watch my sweet sister-in-law with her sleeves rolled high, making pies. She does it so easy—so naturally! I reverence her as I gaze. Often I long for just a teenty bit of pie crust to make a little pie all my own and then sit down in a corner and gobble it up all by myself; but I never ask for I know 'twould bother.

Of an evening she sits by and watches me with a sweet motherly smile while I paste pictures in my scrap-book. She wonders—wonders and ponders me in her heart, then turns with a wholly contented look to where her "dearest, darling husband" sits reading his paper. By and by I kiss them good night and toddle off to bed to leave her telling of my cute little sayings and tricks during the day. And all the time unbeknown to them, I'm "mothering" them in my heart, smiling a little behind it all; sorrowing when I foresee the sorrow *they* cannot, for after all *they* are only children and half of them, I know, forget to say their prayers from sheer happiness, so I have that to do for them though I never have told them of it.

But the next day I'm ready to creep under their wings again for I'm only a lone chick in the world anyway.

It's a peculiar thing to be all alone in the world. You carry your home about in your pocket and wherever you happen to light, there you set it up. When you leave you have just a trunk to pack, your heart to tear up wherever it's taken root, a little sentiment to knock in the head, some idols to break, some memories to smuggle away in the Holy of your heart, and then you set out and if you're wise you burn all behind you. It's lucky for you if you do not take root easily. As for me, I can never be in a place twenty-four hours but that my heart begins reaching out little feelers for something to cling to, and before I'm aware of it, it has taken a grip on the soil about it and "There am I, Caia," and that is "home."

Any old bench, any old tree, that I see for a number of days, becomes dear to me, and so it is I'm always having to break my own heart strings, for I cannot go about the world carrying just any old thing I happen to see, for my trunk and my pockets are both small, and as for my heart, that is already full to bursting.

When I leave this home of mine I know just how 'twill be. I'll want to take the whole room with me, all excepting the wall paper, which must have been designed in a well favored year when crops were full and the harvest plenteous, for such a profusion of wheat as is lying around loose all over its surface I never saw before.

One glimpse of this paper was enough to abolish forever all my vain longings for a dainty girlish room "in cream and pale blue" like the Journal girls have.

I saw clearly that the only effect I could produce would be one of wild picturesqueness, an effect that would cause visitors to bulge their eyes and hold onto their chairs for dear life.

There was a red brick chimney reaching from ceiling to floor and entirely without ornament. I felt my heart sink as I gazed at it, and yet, I was glad to find one oasis in all that desert of wheat, glad there was one spot where grain wouldn't grow.

Oh, if only my ancestors had handed down to me their old oaken chests of silken fabrics and brocaded gowns— then how gracefully I could drape that chimney, after the manner of our day!

But in our family there is only one chest, only one, and strange to say, I have never yet lifted its cover. There are rumors regarding its contents, rumors of a pair of old blue overalls, of a jumper and one cowhide boot, and somehow, although it's in plain view in the garret at home, yet I've never cared to open it. Of course I put no faith in those old rumors, for we all know that it contains a beautiful white brocaded gown and a dainty pair of white slippers!

Thinking of these things set me to dreaming that day, and for half an hour I stood with a far away look in my eyes. But what a shock it is, after one has been wandering in Dreamland in the neighborhood of old oak chests, to suddenly run smack up against a red brick chimney!

I felt that something must be done at once. But what?

Blessed be memory! What a joy it was to remember that down in the bottom of my trunk was an old tin box filled full to the cover with pictures that I had devastated magazines galore in quest of. These were "Stars" and "Leading Women" and women who weren't so leading—no matter—just so they were pictures. I hadn't seen fit to give them a place in the sacred pages of my scrap book, for *that* was to be handed down through the ages. But at last I had a place for them. I mounted a chair with glee and a bottle of glue and pasted them over that chimney: hit or miss, sink or swim, catch on where you can!

When it was finished and I stood looking up at it my brain turned a summer-set off into space. "Too much wine," I muttered, for one of the Stars stood on her head and waved her slippered feet on high, while a "Leading Woman with Jones" lay on her nose and a maid with flowing locks hung on by one toe. Oh, it was pitiful! And yet, these pictures were serving the same purpose the originals do; help to cover the red bricks of reality with the glamour of romance. I knew they never would waken me with a shock from my dreams, and so I said "it was good," and I forsook not the work of my hands.

If I were describing the dresser in this room to a girl chum back east, I should say it was of white teakwood, most beautifully carved, but as it's you I'm talking to, why, I'll tell you truly that this dresser is undoubtedly composed of equal parts of dry-goods boxes and white paint. I cracked the glass trying to insert pictures round its rim like The Journal girls do, so I had to tie up a bouquet of last year's leaves and berries and allow it to trail gracefully down the spinal column of the crack. Together with the pictures and the bouquet there isn't much room left for *me*, but everything goes for art's sake. Sometimes I almost fall into hysterics trying to see something besides my left ear and the sou'west corner of my chin, yet, I never, never remove those decorations.

The bed is of like material to the dresser, but honestly, I don't care what it's made of, just so it isn't a parlor sofa nor a berth in a state-room.

By my chair stands a little bamboo table, and thereby hangs a tail. This tail is just one of my neck ribbons that I have cast away in a moment of frenzy. I cannot say, for certain, what else is on that table for I don't know. But I have my suspicions! I have my suspicions that somewhere below the surface my pocket-book lies bleeding, and from keen observation and patient research I believe the upper stratum to be composed of—books, honey, ink, loaf of bread, flowers, catalogues, and a large dictionary on which a giant chocolate pot wobbles about in reckless glee, seemingly oblivious of all danger. By its side a little souvenir cup hangs on for dear life.

Most visitors look longest at the table, though some of them never turn their eyes from the actress column. One old lady, pointing to the chimney, asked me if I did it. I told her yes, and she then advised me to go out into society more, she said anybody would get morbid living so much in rooms.

She looked wildly around at the wheat fields and the chimney, and the bamboo table; she wrung my hand with tears in her eyes and then left me, feeling for all the world like poor Ruth of old,

"When, sick for home, she stood in tears amid the alien corn."

(Only mine was alien *wheat*.)

I'm thankful there are windows in my room, big enough to cover a big piece of the sky, for the sky, whether in gray or drab or in "cream and pale blue" is always pretty and in good taste.

For the past month the letters from my relatives have begun and ended with this despairing cry: "Tell us *more* about yourself—more, more!"

Even *my* vast and awful egotism fails to supply their demand and there's not enough about me to go half way around.

Sometimes I have to make up things in self defense. Then again I'm forced to go off on a long trip, just so I will have "more about myself" to write to my ravenous kin-folks. That is why I went on the excursion to Victoria, B. C. It wasn't to celebrate the Queen's birthday that I went, for though I like her ever so much, still, you all know how wrapped up I am in the Star Spangled Banner! I didn't go for pleasure either, as most of the poor deluded mortals did, but purely and simply for experience. I hoped the boat would *almost* sink, or that accidentally I'd fall overboard and *almost* drown. I wanted to be sea sick. Which want was speedily gratified and I had all the sea sickness I could hold. Once I had more.

I had thought what a lovely opportunity I should have for studying human nature, and how I'd sit on deck and watch the waves and feel poetical and sweet, and then, next day, what beautiful letters would be homeward bound! How I would delight the souls of my kin with thrilling adventures and poetic flights! But it was not to be so. I just crept away into my state-room the instant we struck the ocean swell, and I lay huddled up in a corner of my berth, saying, "Oh, dear! Oh, dear!" I said this about twenty times or more, for sea-sickness isn't conducive to originality, and I don't believe the wickedest sinner living could have gotten up spunk enough to swear. I turned my pillow over and sobbed on a cold spot; then I had to sit up to let it dry. Out on deck I could hear the minstrel band playing "Nellie Gray," and the lump in my throat grew bigger and bigger, till by and by—I fed the fishes.

When I stood again on my own home shore I felt like hugging the first thing I saw, but I didn't, because it was a telegraph pole. In my room I stood still and feasted my eyes on the old familiar things, and there was no bitterness in my heart that day as I gazed at the fields of wheat—I was so madly thankful to think that paper wasn't covered with millions of little steam-boats. (It might have been, you know) That night I prayed for the fishes and the crocodiles and the poor sailor boys and everything else that is on the sea or beneath the sea or anywhere near the sea.

Of course next day I was sick—not sick like I used to be when mother tucked the bed clothes in and shook the pillows for me and all I had to do was lie and watch the fire through half closed eyes; when there was lovely tea in a sweet, blue cup and toast on a dainty plate; and when I had a dear long legged brother to run those same legs off bringing books to me from the city library; while the neighbors came in with jelly and jam and if, sometimes, they talked me into a fever—no matter, it showed they cared for me. There was a dear old doctor, too, whose words were law and gospel, and if he said castor-oil then castor-oil went.

Now, I abominate doctors, both male and female. They come in and strut 'round the room and puff and talk and gag you with a thermometer and then they say in a loud, hilarious voice, that "what *you* need, young lady, is cheering up."

You lie still with every nerve on edge and a hatred in your heart for that man which would no doubt surprise him if he knew of it—but he don't—he's too busy "cheering you up."

Someone just knocked: it was a girl selling volumes on "Our Late War with Spain."

I groaned, but not out loud, for

there was something in the wistful expression of her eyes that went straight through my heart. I told her gently that I didn't care for warbooks, but when I saw the light die out of her eyes, why, I changed my mind and ordered one. The light came back to her face in a jiffy and she said *so* hopefully that that made the third order she'd taken since morning. I wanted to cry—it wasn't pity, but I just couldn't help thinking how I'd feel if I was in her shoes. I may have overdone my sympathy, and yet, when I remember that little thin face and those eyes that could grow hopeful because, forsooth, their owner had taken three whole orders in one long day—when I remember this, I don't think I've wasted any of my precious, good-for-nothing sympathy.

But perhaps she has pleasures that are only memories to you and me; perhaps to-night when she trudges home there'll be a mother waiting for her and they'll sit in the fire-light and plan and dream dreams for the future. Oh, if I thought she had a mother I'd be sorry I didn't buy two books. 'Though I really couldn't afford it. I struggle so hard to save something! Last week I saved fifty cents out of my daily food fund and by Saturday noon I was so hungry I had to go down town and order a regular Sarah T. Rohrer dinner, whole wheat bread and all. That cost me thirty-five cents, and the remainder I blowed in for chocolate drops.

Life is all a struggle, say what you will. If strife and wrestling with one's self and everybody else developes character then mine must be a whopper; and if broken resolutions *do* pave the way to Chicago then my pavement must be nearly done.

Every night I make tremendous programmes for the following day, in which every minute is accounted for, every hour has its work. On the morrow, to a casual observer, it would seem as if I were straining every nerve to do as exactly the opposite thing as possible.

I bite off so much more than I can chew that it keeps me busy all day long, spitting it out again.

When one has a cold and a head big as a pumpkin and eyes that shed briny drops without any provocation whatever, and when this one is trying to compose sentences and write them down between sneezes, with what agony of soul does this afflicted being hear foot-steps approaching and then a loud knock on the door!

Reader, often and often I am such a tortured one. I hear a knock; I grab myself by the arm and by main force drag my body to the door; I open it and grin at the person standing there. This person smiles back with a sunshiny radiance in her face that is fairly blinding. She says she came to call—that she'd just been trying all week long to come for she knew how dreadfully lonely I must be

(I'm still grinning). She next remarks that she sees I've been writing a letter, and adds that if I'm anything like her I'm glad enough to be interrupted.

My heart cries out that I'm not like her, never was and never want to be, but my heart can't cry above a whisper, so the caller doesn't hear. She smiles and chats and gossips and has a lovely time all by herself, while I grin on. I know now, why skeletons grin so perpetually. They hate to hurt peoples' feelings and so they pretend they're having a high old time. Well, they have my sympathy and pretty soon I'll join their joyous band if callers don't stop coming when I've got a cold. Of course it depends a great deal on who the caller is. Now, if *you*, dear reader, should ever come, I'd be tickled to death. Only whatever you do, don't say you s'pose I'm dreadfully lonesome. I tell you I'm never really lonesome excepting on such great occasions as the

Fourth o' July when I'm down town watching the parade, or else on circus day or, well, last Sunday I was lonely as I sat in a crowded street car that was carrying home from church a burden of noble ladies, who shook their trailing gowns and rustled their purple and fine linen and spread themselves over more seat than I could ever occupy lying at full length. There was one girl so pretty! But somehow the more I looked at her the lonesomer I grew, and when her mamma gazed over my head with a pale contraction of her aristocratic mouth, why, *then*, if you'd have mentioned my lonely state I'd have wept on your neck and begged you to stop the car and take me away. I don't resent sympathy when I really need it but it's just when I'm happy and contented that I hate being pitied—that's all.

I *do* wish the *wrong* people wouldn't be good to me. I mean that I wish folks who are wicked sinners wouldn't bring me in a nice plate of fresh rolls for my supper.

There's a woman in this building does that and those rolls are good. Every time before eating them I resolve never to accept another thing from her, but after I've devoured two or three of them, I somehow can't help feeling that there must be some good in her after all, and perhaps it's my mission in life to bring it out.

Her sins are not so many but a few. Firstly, she was heard to laugh three months after her husband's death. Secondly, she has a sweet, winning smile which (Thirdly) caused a young man to fall deeply in love with her. And this young man (Fourthly) had been keeping company with the daughter of the gen'leman who owns this building, and now this daughter (Fifthly) is growing very thin so that she only weighs one hundred and eighty pounds. Those are the reasons why (Sixthly) I should avoid said woman and said rolls.

A little girl coming home from school has set me to thinking of the days of yore and the girl I've left behind me.

I have never spoken of her much for she was just a mere school girl, unknown to the world, and yet, she bore my name and I loved her very dearly for many years. I hated to give her up and so I kept her dresses above her shoe-tops and her hair done in a pig tail long, long after the younger fry were flaunting their young ladies' gowns and wearing their locks in a Psyche. I hung on to her for dear life but Grim Old Time hung harder and so she passed away with my school days.

By schooldays I mean all those days that lived and had their being before the college came to town. Oh, that college, that busy, blustering institution with its stern-eyed Profs., who marched in army-like array through the sacred halls; who banged the silent doors, shattered the Lares and Penates and seemingly crushed out all the traditionary sentiment that clung to the old Academy.

These Profs. never knew your name nor who you were. They called you Miss Green and Miss Brown and Miss Jones from morning till night and were forever mistaking you for someone you hated like poison. Our little customs and individualities were trampled on as rudely as if we were in the grasp of the old Norman Conquerors. They placed wall-eyed preps. in the time worn seats that were ours in the days when teachers were our best friends and knew us almost as well as our mothers did, and when our seat-mates were dearer than relations. How the whole school would roar if you said a funny thing, or if, on a Friday, you forgot your piece, then the girls would all gather around you and tell you not to mind, and they'd enumerate the many, many times they'd "broke down and never cared a single bit."

The love I bore for my studies was a peculiar sort of love. I never demonstrated it by study or high rank in class or in examination. Oh, no! Many a girl with the odor of the high school still clinging to her frock, whose lessons were mere drudgery, stood fathoms above me. But I didn't mind. I always had a knack of going my own sweet way. Just the sight of the covers of my old Cæsar would bring a smile to my face and my Literature books would set me off at Dreamland. They were always so full of suggestions, and for me, their greatest charm lay in the reading between the lines.

(There was one book whose covers I didn't care much for. I generally kept it completely out of sight for one sniff of that Algebra would give me the jim-jams for a month.)

But over the grave of the Old Academy the New College grew and waxed strong. It carried on its traffic, manufactured graduates and sold its wares to the admiring natives.

But when I came to leave it after a time, I was a very surprised little girl to find how much I loved it; it was with great wonder that I felt a mighty pain at my heart as I realized, too late, what a jolly, dear old place it was after all. There was something in the warm-hearted grasp of its hand and the motherly smile it shed on me at parting that reminded me, strangely enough, of the dear old Academy, and so I forgave it then and there.

There's nobody I love to have come so well as the onion lady. She cheers my stomach as well as my heart.

She was in a little while ago. She gave me one look and then she said: "Why, child alive, you're looking dreadfully peaked. Are you sure you eat the right kind of food?"

"The *right* kind!" I sobbed, "why, *any* kind would taste just beautiful and make me strong and well." And a big tear fell off my chin and I moaned piteously as I told her how I hadn't had anything since morning but a teaspoonful of Hood's Sarsaparilla.

She groaned, and taking me by the arm led me into her cozy rooms.

In half an hour I was sitting opposite her at the daintiest of tables. It might have been because she asked the blessing, or else the dear way she had of waiting on me, or the little blue cups of tea, or maybe just because I was so hungry—but anyhow it was the loveliest meal I've had since long 'fore *you* were born.

She told me all about her daughter whose picture hangs over the mantle. A sweet, innocent, girlish face smiling as only eighteen *can* smile.

I saw the cheery light die out of My Lady's eyes and a quiver stir her mouth as she looked at it, for her daughter is not dead but married, and she is married to the "wrong one." Poor little girl, I could have told her long ago that whoever she married he'd be the wrong one, because all the right ones have been dead these many thousand years.

"Not dead, but sleeping," say you?

"Well, if that is the case, for mercy sakes walk softly, shut the door gently and don't wake them up, for if you wake one of them up out of a snooze he'll be uglier than seven bears for a week.

Someday he'll wake up of his own accord.

Someday——

"When the Sun is cold
And the Stars are old,
And the leaves of the judgment-book
 unfold."

Then he'll sit up in bed with a start and he'll think somebody has run a hot pin through him. Not that anybody really will, but it'll just be his own conscience pricking him. But I can't talk on such a theme any longer —no use trying—I haven't the patience. My fingers just itch to get hold of a jolly nice long hat-pin. I could wield it with glee long, long in advance of that day when the judgment-book unfolds. Yea, Young Man, even *now!*

Though I'm seldom lonely I'll own up that there are days in my existence I'd just as soon skip. But maybe you've heard before that life isn't a story book whose leaves can be turned over a dozen in a bunch, whose stupid parts may be skipped at will and only the interesting portions read? Life is another kind of a book. Every mortal page of it must be waded through. We spell out the minutes and hesitate and stammer over the long, long hours, wishing as fiercely for the end as if we were reading a chapter in old Webster.

On such days, the instant I open my eyes in the morning, I'm sorry, and I continue in this sorrow through the whole day.

After breakfast I take a spin on my wheel, but I don't spin long for just as I'm fairly under headway, nature waveth her magic wand and the demons of the wind are let loose on my track. My vail floats away on the wings of the morning and my sailor rests lovingly on my left ear, while all the wealth of my tan colored tresses mingles with my eye-winkers. I finally give one heart rending wobble and there's a wreckage on corner of Pike and 2nd, or on James and 1st, or any other of the main traveled streets of the city. I scramble up wildly for fear of being lugged off in the patrol. I don't ride any more that day but I go home and write a letter as follows:

At Home,
May 30, '99.

Dearest and ownliest friend:—
I just now received your loving letter. (Reader, I received that letter about two weeks ago.) I was so glad to get it! I do hope your finger wasn't cut very bad. Did you put a rag on it? If you didn't you must do it at once. (That finger was cut about three weeks previous to the writing of this letter.)

I went for a bike ride this morning—had a lovely time. (Reader you have already heard of that ride.)

Oh, I wish you were here with me!

(no, I don't quite, because she talks a mile a second and eats everything!)

How is your mama and your papa and your little sister and your auntie and your grandmother? Is your cousin better now! I do hope so. (She hasn't got any cousin at all now—he's been dead a long, long while.)

Be sure and give your mama and your papa and your little sister my love, and your grandmother and auntie too— also your cousin.

I have some new tan shoes. They are just lovely and *so* easy on my feet! (Reader, those shoes have almost pinched my toes to a jelly.)

Well I must close as the postman will soon be here to gather up the letters. (The postman doesn't come for three hours yet.)

Give my love to all, keeping a large chunk for yourself. As ever your old friend and school-mate,   ABBIE.

This finished I feel that I ought to write to my brothers and sisters and other relations, but oh, I love them too much to send down upon them such an epistle as the above.

Then one of the girls I know calls, and my heart thrills with hope. But no, she can't stay! Mama just sent her up to ask me if I had any nice book to read.

I feel like recommending Spurgeon's Sermons to her but I refrain, and instead I resurrect some old dog-eared novel and give it to her with a muttered blessing.

When blessed evening comes at last I lower the shades, freshen the fire and draw the little bamboo table close to the old sofa where I cuddle up in a heap, with a dozen books at my side and a cup of chocolate delicately balancing itself on the highest point of the bamboo table. I sip this chocolate from time to time. I open first one book and then another, but they weary me. 'Til at the bottom of the pile I find an old worn book my mother used to like, and I open it at a certain chapter about being "weary with my groaning all the day long." It just suits me and it's such a comfort to know that a long time ago there was a king named David who felt like "Weary Willie" too, sometimes.

I read Psalm after Psalm and they all fit my case precisely. I tell you that old song book David wrote so long ago comes in pretty good sometimes.

When I have bilious spells brought on by too rich reading; when my mouth tastes of current periodicals and measles, and my stomach craves startling high spiced foods in the form of Modern Novels, then it is that I like Saul can be soothed by nothing but one of David's songs.

Poor old Saul! I expect he used to sit up nights reading about "Our Late War" till he got the jim jams in both legs.

May, being the month of apple blossoms and also the month of my birth, I have a special love for her. But she has disappointed me this year. She has caused the rain to fall on the just and the unjust alike till the Indians have prophesied a cold and rainy summer and the ravens have croaked and the wise men wagged their heads.

However, just at last she has proved

herself human; after giving us thirty days of rain and wind, lo! on the thirty-first day of her reign she has repented her—not in sack-cloth and ashes, but in sunshine and blue sky. She couldn't bear to slip into the eternity of the past with all the burden of those rainy days upon her soul; couldn't bear to leave behind her not one sunshiny day for us to remember her by, and so, with a shrewd insight into the human heart she chose the very last day for her face to shine in. Just as some of our friends who have treated us shabby for a month, turn 'round and are just melting good for about two hours before they set sail for Honolulu. They leave some parting gift in our hand and kiss us and cry on us and behold, how we love them! Their kindly smile *and* the little gift which maybe cost two or three dollars, has wiped out the whole bitter past. We remember no more the night when they rolled up in the bed clothes and wouldn't budge an inch. Forgotten is that hour of agony when we hung suspended in the space between the bed and floor, while our friends lay peacefully snoozing in our place—and then, when the final crash came and our head was pillowed on the floor matting we remember no longer how these same friends sat up in bed and cried out saying:

"Well, I never! If you haven't *actually* tumbled out of bed!"

Yes, we've forgotton all this and we hope our friends will have a lovely time in Honolulu—and stay a long, long time.

Really and truly I do think that rent in this man's town is enormous. The sum of money that passes every month in advance, into the clutches of the gen'leman who owns (Oh, you know the rest!) is dreadful to relate. I shan't tell how much *my* rent is, for some of my friends, I know, would be shocked at my dire extravagance while others who are millionaires, semi-millioniares and quarti-millionaires, would sniff their nostrils in disdain at such a mere nothing. But I guess if their little tin bank was filled with just mere nothings, they'd sniff out the other side of their nose. If I were a millionaire I know what I'd do. After five or six years I'd die off and leave everything to some nice young lady who was struggling to keep a roof over her.

I'm afraid if you were here you'd tell me I ought to give up these rooms and go in search of cheaper ones. But don't, *don't* do it; don't set the poor old stone to rolling again so soon! Do you think that I could bear to leave this chimney, this little bamboo table, the dresser of teak-wood and the real bed that is *not* a sofa! Do you think I could leave all this and go wandering about the highways and hedges in search of a room that at best, would be but one dollar cheaper? No, rather will I save on my butcher bill, which will be quite easy as I don't eat meat. I'm what you'd call a vegetarian, that is, I would be, only I don't eat vegetables either; I just take Hood's Sarsaparilla three times a day for that weary Willie feeling in my head.

I'm getting a little thin, and that reminds me: I met the minister's wife the other day—who is *not* getting thin. I almost knew she'd say something to make me hate her again, and sure enough! She gazed at me a moment with her peculiar eyes and then remarked that it seemed to her I was looking terribly *puny*. That word! The very same one that hung like a pall over my happy childhood, darkening and embittering it.

You see, when I was a little girl about seven years old, I lived in the country. And there was an old doctor who went about from house to house, selling catnip tea and balsam. One night, just at supper, he honored us with a visit. He was sitting opposite me at table, when suddenly he turned to my mother, and pointing vividly at me in the presence of all my relations, he said in a loud voice: "Mark my words, Madam, that child is puny, terribly puny."

I gave him one look of intense hatred. I saw my brothers smile with glee, and well did I know that omen of ill!

After that, whenever I wanted to go hunting or skating or play "robber" or ride old Bill or slide on the new sled or play in the loft,—no matter what—those boys would gurgle with fiendish delight and say with mock sorrow:

"Nope sis, we're awful sorry we can't take you, but you're puny, you know, terribly puny."

When I had measles and whooping cough they would gather about my bed and ask in gentle tones if I wasn't feeling pretty puny to-day.

In time I developed a fierce thick frown. I cried out for folks to "let me be" and for "them boys not to talk to me." I learned to go about with an independent air, and every one knew, from the look in my eye, that 'twas "none o' their business." I would sit for hours on an old log over the creek, swinging my legs and smiling an uncanny smile as I dreamed how, some fine morning, I'd run away to a far off land and teach school till I had money enough to buy a gold watch set with rubies and a pink silk dress like the girl in the calendar had. And then, by and by, when I was eighteen and all the family had gathered together in the old farm house to mourn my loss; when all the aunts and uncles who had ever patronized me and all the cousins who had broken my dolls, came from afar to weep with one another—then in all my magnificence I would open the door and step in upon them, and the prodigal family would fall on my neck and weep and ask my forgiveness and then go and kill the fatted turkey. (No fatted calf in mine, if you please.)

During those days, and ever since, my friends have wagged their heads and muttered how they feared I never should care for anybody. Unless, as my Cousin Jane once whispered in my ear, unless he was the "right one"—some one, you understand, who would be fearfully, madly, wildly homely, with lines of sorrow about his mouth and—*smart*, he must be smart, she said. Why Jane should think I have a predilection for ugliness and smartness is more than I can surmise, for you yourselves know how I love pretty things, and as for smartness, why, there's nobody who cares less for it. Nobody who enjoys common ordinary folks more than I do, folks who never have even heard of Darwin's theory and don't know Browning from a hole in the ground. Who will innocently ask me how to spell "it" or "but," and if I don't exactly know they like me all the better for it and don't act as if I'd committed murder in the first degree. Sometimes they will look up from a book and enquire of me what "expectation" means. I look thoughtful a moment and then announce that "expectation is when anybody expects something every day for a month and then don't get it." This mayn't be just as Webster would put it but I don't care, it appeals to my people and they understand it. They know it's true from experience, and lots of times I've had my definitions bring tears to their eyes and they'd weep as they told me how often *they* had felt exactly that way.

Of course one of Webster's definitions will bring tears to one's eyes also, but they are tears of saltpeter and carbolic acid and are vastly different from the crystal drops of tenderness that flow from the human heart at hearing one of *my* definitions.

If I ever *do* write a dictionary I'm going to write one that will make men and women better for having read it—not better intellectually, but truer and kinder and nobler at heart. But I'd hate to have to define a bicycle track. The most I know about it is that I'm not caring anything about riding on one. I enjoyed it once away back in January when cycling was out of season and the track was out of repair. I don't know what prompted me to ride that day, for it had rained the night before and the track was decidedly soggy, while the air was full of a soft oozy mist. The track leads to a little lake some six or seven miles away—if I were only good at description, which we all know I'm not, I'd give you a vivid picture of it; but let it suffice to say that it is crooked and narrow and goes sidling 'round and 'round and over and above and through a collection of hills; there are dark and bloody gulches and terrible precipices, but withal there is bewilderingly beautiful scenery everywhere. My heart thrilled with delightful uncertainty as, ever and anon, I came upon a point where a jutty of the hill made a sudden curve in the path, and what was around that curve was as hidden as the future; it might be a grizzly bear or a—man! I went along at an easy gait, now catching sweet glimpses of the little lake far below, now peering up into mossy gulches, till suddenly I came upon a shady nook wherein was a small bench. It undoubtedly had been "built for two" but I found that *one* could occupy it very comfortably without feeling lonely at all. My lunch too, I discovered, was about right for one—in fact, I didn't see how I could possibly have been hospitable to two of us.

Lunches are all right in their place but that place is not the human stomach, they leave one with such an unhealthy craving for drink, also with a lump in one's throat, composed of two boiled eggs, one pickle, one sandwich and a piece of roll jelly cake. I looked about for water; but even when I found it what did it avail me? There was no cup to go with it, not even an old rusty dipper with a hole in it!

And I'm not one of those children of nature who can lie flat down and drink from a running stream. Not that I'm afraid of getting my dress muddy nor of doing anything ungentlemanly, but simply because just as a big cool draught goes careering down my throat I imagine there are other things likewise careering down it, such as big, cool snake eggs, large, wet spiders; and when, suddenly, a great damp green toad hops up on the opposite bank, on a level with my eyebrows, and waves his little toes at me —oh it's horrible!

So it was that I stood there helpless beside the running brooklet. The eggs were petrifying in my throat and I could locate the exact place where the pickles lay. Then my eyes espied the eggshells. I snatched thirstily at the half of one and took my station by the beautiful stream. I drank and drank and drank again, till the burden of my throat rolled away.

I mounted my wheel once again, but from there on the path grew more dangerous, the curves more numerous and sudden, while every rod or so a white sign-board hopped up by the track, saying loudly: "Ring your bell!" "Go slow!" "Keep to the right!"

I am convinced that these sign-boards do more harm than good, for they caused my wheel to shy fearfully, and to whizz round the curves like blue lightning. And as for ringing the bell, there was no need of it, for I was monarch of all that beautiful path, and never a fellow biker did I meet the whole way.

Foolish child that I was, I thought it would always be so, thought I could come there next June and find the same sweet quietude, thought I could ride along there at the same ambling gate, sit on the old bench and eat my lunch and drink from the little stream just as I did that day in January. And it was with a feeling of joyful expectation that I sallied forth, bound for the track, one morning not far away. I don't remember much about that ride—I just have a confused recollection of hundreds of people whizzing by one another as if pursued; peering into one another's faces with wild, eager eyes; ringing their bells like mad; scorching round the curves with set faces and glaring eyes! Few and short the words they said, few and short the thoughts they thunk!

Maybe the little lake was still there below, and the trees and the bench by the quiet stream, but I didn't see them. I saw nothing but whirring wheels and pantings and puffings and ringing of bells; felt nothing but a fierce desire to "go it" with the rest —go it till I died.

I own up to it that one experiences a certain wild fascination such as a locomotive must feel as it goes ripping and snorting over the plains and the mountains.

And to certain individuals I've no doubt it's beneficial. To such as have feasted on sentiment till there's nothing left but bones; who have wrung their hands in rapture over the sunset, and cried their eyes red gazing at the moon; whose thoughts were bred in an incubator and whose feelings were purchased "ready made" —oh, I should think they *would* want to ride a million miles a minute to see if they couldn't get away from themselves. Let them mount their wheels in hot haste and make for the track where all they'll need will be muscle and brawn and strength of limb—and a license on their wheel.

But as for me, give me a smooth old country road, with maybe a rut here and there or maybe a little hill— who cares for things like these? All is quiet there. Perhaps there'll be no lake, no beautiful scenery, but almost always there's a quiet stream or a shady pool with willows all around, and then—there is time, all the time in the world: time to watch a cloud drift by, or stop at a farm house and ask for a drink; and plenty of time to think the thoughts that only come to one in such sweet, simple places as these. You amble along the old white road meeting nothing worse than a cow or lumber wagon, with a kind old face smiling down at you from the high spring seat. I'd love to follow the road on to the end, for I know they'd be good to me, the people who live by its highways and hedges.

The cows might shake their moosey heads at me, but by the time they had fairly whetted their horns, I should be skimming over yonder hill. I might meet some poor Wandering Jew who, like myself, had found his best friend to be the old country road. But I shouldn't be afraid, for I know he'd recognize in me something akin to himself, and he'd give me a dusty grin and pass on without so much as staying his weary feet to question my purpose or my purse.

The trouble would be, when in my course I came upon some little hamlet the natives of which would gather together on the street corners and eye me suspiciously.

"Why," they would ask, "why is this being who sitteth upon a bike, riding through space in this wise? It cannot be for pleasure, for the creature is alone. Let us hasten up and question her."

They would ask, did I ride for money?

And I would answer, no!

Did I ride for fame?

Again, no!

Did I ride for duty?

No!

Then what in Bryan's name *was* I riding for?

And I should smile a sweet shy smile, touch the spur to my trusty bike and leave them rubbing their eyes with their knubby fists. For why should I parley with them? If I told them my real reason they would only mock me and look down their Judas noses: if I said, "Fellow laborers and friends! I am riding through space in this manner, not for fame, not for money, not from a sense of duty but merely because I *want* to," they would either think me insane or else a Cuban spy.

Oh, hum! Let's go home. For home is *home* even if it *is* just a dry goods box in an alley or a room in a block.

"I suppose this seems like home to you," said a friend of mine one day. "I suppose it doesn't seem lonely or dreary or—or horrible to you?"

And she gazed about while a shiver crept up her back—not that I saw it but it was in the room and the very air was charged with it.

I told her I managed to exist here.

But honestly now, didn't I think

I'd be happier if I'd take up embroidery or sewing or something; hadn't I ever thought of learning millinery or anything? I should be so much more contented, she thought, if I had something to take up my mind.

To hear her talk anybody would think I had a face on me like Dante, with the light of Inferno in my eyes, and a lover lost in our late war, while my mind was a regular Sahara desert and my soul a Dakota plain.

When she'd gone away I felt so unhappy, with my thoughts in a tangle and with a miserable fear at my heart that maybe, after all, I was on the wrong side of the river, and that the folks on the other bank were having the best time. But just as the tears were filling my eyes a big burst of sun came through my window, filling my lap full of sunshine, while a stray verse came singing into my heart and I fell to humming in undertone:

"There's a joy in mere existence
That the raptured soul consumes."

And then I took a deep breath of sunshine, laughed drowsily, curled up on the sofa and fell asleep.

There's one thing I've never been and that's a school teacher. I have always humored myself in thinking that someday I'd be one, someday when I got far enough along in my 'rithmetic.

But honestly, I believe if it came to a pinch and I had to choose between *that* and going as missionary to the Cannibal Islands, I'd take the missionary every time.

It just makes my tooth jump to think of having some little curly-headed infant toddle up to my desk and ask me through its little nose where the Philippines were. "Pa said fer me to ask *you*."

And just to think of some tall, fair haired Maid of Athens in a pink calico apron, stalking up to me and entreating me to show her how to work an example in partial payments, and then to have her stand and look over my shoulder through the whole business!

Every time I beheld a little grimy hand raised on high I'd faint dead away for I'd be sure they were going to ask some abominable question their Pa had set them up to.

I suppose that every woman at some time of her life, ought to don a white apron and tie on her sunbonnet and trudge through the fields and over the hill to the little old school house down in the hollow.

I had a teacher once, and if I thought I'd ever be loved by any morsel of human flesh as *that* teacher was loved by me, why I'd furbish up my arithmetic and teach school for the rest of my days.

I adored her; her lovely brown eyes and the long braid of hair that hung down her back. The day she picked me up and kissed me was a day to be remembered.

I would plod through the snow in winter till I was worn out with trying to walk in the footsteps of my long-legged brothers—footsteps, oh, how few and far between and how like giant post holes! But it was worth while enduring all this just to have that dear teacher untie my hood and hold me on her lap for an hour. And if she ever winked knowingly over my head at my big brothers, I never saw her.

Sometimes I stayed all night with her and once she showed me her beautiful dresses and another time she brought forth a little box full of "keepsakes," she called them. There was a penny and a heart candy; a button and a picture, a lock of hair and an old thimble, etc. I looked at them with awe; they opened up a new vista of life to me, an undiscovered country. Keepsakes! Why, *I* didn't have any, but you bet I would before another day was past.

I went home. I found a button box and I cut off all the brass buttons from two pairs of pants. I swiped my mother's thimble and some pennies from the boys, and as for hair, I cut a lock off the head of every member of the family, from my oldest brother down to my little dog Gip.

The next time the teacher stayed at our house for tea, with what pride did I show her *my* box! Nobody smiled, nobody laughed. But she just said it was every bit as nice as hers, and held me on her lap the whole evening. And I know she did *not* wink at the boys either—now!

You needn't say she was good to me just because of them either, for I know better, and I tell you I *will not* have this idol broken.

Talk about worshiping idols! Jimminy Christmas! I'd like to see anybody get a chance to worship one. You no sooner get your nice little idol set up than somebody comes along with a hammer and smashes it to splinters and tells you it's no good anyhow, that its feet are of clay, and a whole lot more stuff.

Then you make yourself another one, taking pains with its feet to have them of shiny gold. Somebody comes again. Yes, its feet are all right this time, but now its head is of *pumpkin*. So it goes, and oh dear, I *do* wish folks would let other folks be!

Now I'll talk a little about keepsakes. Little children gathered here to-day, never willfully seek to acquire keepsakes. In their own good time they'll come to you, thicker than measels and they'll stay a great deal longer.

"Till death us do part," I say sadly when another keepsake makes its way into my little desk. Oftentimes I heroically throw away with the rubbish some worthless trinket I'm tired of, but in half an hour's time I'm down searching for it in the ash barrel.

They accumulate in boxes and drawers and always they seem to be saying to me, "Whither thou goest we will go, thy trunk shall be our trunk, *thy* boxes *our* boxes."

The best way to do is to fill your pockets with them, tie a gunny sack full around your neck and another on your back, and then go down to the City Dock and jump off into the Bay.

For me, I suppose the noblest thing to do before making the grand jump of a lifetime, would be to tie up these keepsakes into neat little bundles and send them away to my friends and relations. But would they appreciate them? Supposing I sent Jane a little old cracked cup I've had for years wouldn't she sniff with disdain and give it to little Anna Belle Lee for her play house! And I know if I sent Mary that little souvenir spoon of mine with the battleship Maine, before it went busted, beautifully engraved on its bowl, I know she'd not only sniff with disdain but howl with disgust and say she'd seen the likes of them before and they were brass clear through! She should think I might have sent her something that at least made a pretense of being gold. That dear little brass spoon! how it helps to ladle up the past to me! And the little cracked cup is full to the brim of memories of the giver—even the crack tells a story and brings back other days a hundred times clearer than any old yellow page in a diary could do.

I abominate diaries! The harder you try to make them bright and interesting the stupider and affecteder and sentimentaller they get till finally they are just about as exciting as a tub of rain water seasoned with angle worms. You are supposed to be writing a Diary for no other eye than your own, but the first thing you know you are writing down a whole chapter of sentimental trash and dreaming how Neddie or Johnny or Jimmie will run across it lying on the bench underneath the apple trees and how he'll read therein that you are eating up your heart by the pound all for the love of him, and then how he'll come tearing up the walk on his little chubby legs and fall at your feet crying out that it might have been so different, oh so different, if he'd only have known sooner! And he weeps on his red bandana and you weep on your gingham apron and then he kisses your left ear madly, passionately, and rushes away to inform Susie Green that he loves another and for her to give him back his ring quick.

You can't be true to yourself and write a Diary at the same time.

Being true to one's self reminds me of a little incident fraught with grief and pain.

The classroom was very still. Professor and students were gathered about a long table laden with departed beasts, for lo, it was a Physiology class! Reader, I was there all but my heart and my eyes; they were out picking buttercups in the sweet, clean meadows.

The group about the table were intent upon something the little plump professor held in his hand. I learned afterwards that it was the eye of a cow. This cow never again would roam the green pastures and switch her brindle tail in the sunshine, for her weary bones had been whitening long upon some grassy slope or shady hollow, and only her eye was left to tell the tale. I like cows' eyes—in their place—in a cow's head: provided that same cow is living and breathing and chewing her cud and looking pensively at me with her soft brown orbs —then I think cows' eyes are pretty, but in death — I draw the line. I drew the line that day. As in a dream I realized that they were searching for something on that eyeball. The professor said a little black spot should invariably appear on the something or other of the something or other that belonged to the eye.

At last they all found it, all save *one*!

"There were ninety and nine in the fold that day,
But one was lost on the hills away,"

sounded mournfully in my mind; and, oh reader, *I* was that lost one, for to save my life I couldn't see that wretched little black spot. I gazed and gazed till the class grew impatient and the professor grew irritable. Well, even girls with green eyes and big ears have something of the actress in them. This quality had hitherto lain dormant in me but *now* there was need of it. I clasped my hands; a look of excitement crept into my face and I cried out in an ecstatic voice: "Oh, I see it, I see it! Isn't it a *dear* little spot?" I deceived the class entirely, but not so the wily Prof. My eyes had bulged a trifle too much and the note of ecstacy in my voice had been a trifle too loud for his quick ear to be deceived by it. He looked at me sadly and said: "Miss Abbie, whatever you do, be true to yourself." Then I saw several hundred little black spots and I felt sorry, very, very sorry, for no matter how much I may fib to other folks I've always wanted to be true to myself and do the square thing by it.

But between you and me and my own heart I *do* think I was true to myself, for I saw that black spot as clearly in my *mind's* eye as if I had focused a dozen ordinary green eyes at it.

Of course I shouldn't have called it a "dear" little spot, nor acted tickled about it,—but goodness, I guess anybody would act tickled to see even a Missouri cousin if 'twas in self-defence.

Not long after we stood again in the little class room. It looked like Noah's Ark struck by lightning ten days before.

On the table lay some half dozen cats who had passed quietly away some time ago. There were several dogs slain by an assassin. There were chickens, "absolutely fresh," and little odds and ends in the shape of toads, mice, etc. Oh, the table was just covered with and-so-forths.

I sniffed with anguish and two young ladies grew pale and **wobbly**,. which caused the little Prof. to remark angrily that as for *him, he* could relish his dinner in that same room as much as if he was in his own dining-room at home, (which wasn't saying much for the dining-room at home.)

I looked at him. He had a kind, honest face with nothing hardened in its expression, nothing of depravity in his glance which could lead one to believe in the truth of his remark. I saw that just for his profession's sake he had wheedled himself into believing a wretched lie;.and when I had compared that direful room with his own cool, fresh dining room at home where the white curtains fluttered to and fro, and the china shone on the dainty table, while a sweet little wife poured out tea for him; when I compared these two rooms I said in undertone: "Old man, whatever you do, be true to yourself." You notice I didn't say it out loud, for behold, examinations were nigh at hand and their proximity makes a lot of difference in a body's manner of speaking to his Prof.

Now I think of it, he was exceedingly merciful to me on that day of sorrow. He must have been thinking of other things when he examined my paper and marked it "Passed." When he read about a horse's tail that was t-a-l-e, and when in answer to a question asking for the exact location of the heart he was informed by that same paper that the heart hasn't any special place of staying but that it beats on one side till it gets tired and then flops over to the other.

No doubt his conscience pricked him for passing me, and yet he was being true to himself—to his *best* self you understand. Which doesn't care a picayune *where* a body's heart may be just so it's good and true, and beats in sympathy with some poor flunking student.

But I've no doubt *that* will be among the first sins he confesses on the Great Day. I wouldn't be a bit surprised But just as he's telling how sorry he is for it, wouldn't it be a joke if the ones who are running the thing then should tell him it was one of the very best things he ever did?

There'll be lots of jokes that day I expect—lots of things going on that will make the angels hide behind their wings and smile. Wouldn't it be odd if while I'm confessing how I ate that wicked sinner's rolls, and telling how sorry I am I treated her nice and pleasant, if *then* they'd tell *me* that was one of *my* best deeds?

And when I'm telling about the day I got lost and wandered about till I strayed into the slums—but perhaps I'd better tell the reader about it first. I got lost one day before I had thoroughly learned the lay of the city in which I dwelt, and as lost folks always do, I strayed into the very worst place. But I wasn't at all worried. I was too much interested.

I was remembering all I had ever read about *Slums*, 'specially Dickens' slums. I forgot all about being a young lady: I forgot to hold up my skirt and to pick my way—I even forgot that I had on a beautiful new pair of shoes. I ambled along. On a corner stood an old man. He was swearing—he didn't tell me why but I knew. I knew 'twas just because he was miserable and wicked and poverty stricken. How I wished I could smile as some girls can, then maybe I could have cheered his weary old soul and made him forget to swear for a moment. As it was, my mouth made a pitiful stagger at a smile which ended in a woebegone pucker and my eyes grew watery and. I've no doubt the poor old fellow thought I too, was in trouble, for he swore all the harder at the world present and the world to come and all the inhabitants thereof. I stumbled on till I almost fell over a little—baby(?) I don't know. It might have been a baby if I could have gotten a glimpse of it. Anyhow it had a baby's eyes: pitiful, beseeching. I didn't try to smile for I was beyond even a meager grin. I longed to be a big strong man so I could put the little creature bodily into my coat pocket and carry it home to my wife and have her clean it all up and feed it and then— what then? Oh, surely there'd be room somewhere in this world for a sweet clean baby!

I stood there perfectly helpless. My hands weren't strong nor my heart wasn't strong, and then besides, missionaries are born not made.

Then by mere chance I staggered into the light of day and the bustle and noise of a civilized street. I held up my skirt from the dust in a hurry, and straightened my hat and looked with chagrin at the mire on my shoes. I reached my room feeling very much ashamed and I sent up a prayer for forgiveness then and there. I promised to cleanse my linen skirt from mud and my new tan shoes from contaminating clay. I wonder if the angels laughed in heaven and if, on the Day when we're all there—not in heaven, I don't mean—I wonder if they'll tell me that they don't deal in young ladies and linen skirts and new tan shoes, and the only prayer they remember of hearing from me that day was the one I prayed unconsciously, a prayer without words that came straight from my heart as I passed the old man in the slums, and the little baby, having forgotten myself for just one little moment.

I only wish I knew how to read a newspaper. One is delivered every evening at my domicile door but to save my life I can't get into it. Just as I'm beginning to be a little bit interested in some harmless advertisement suddenly a great heavy line of brazen letters rises up before me and startles me so I can hardly make out its meaning. After gazing intently at it for half an hour I discover its purpose to be,

"She shot her husband and then killed herself. Jealously the alleged motive."

These heavy lines are called "headers" I think, and they make me feel as I do when a hot-tamalie fiend yells in my ear.

Generally newspapers do not acquire pulpit methods, but they evidently have adopted the custom of ancient ecclesiastics who were wont to talk softly and gently in a low undertone for about fifteen minutes, and then suddenly, without any warning whatever, begin roaring, stamping and waving their arms till anybody would think they were trying to shout down the walls of Jericho.

"A man died in Philadelphia," last night's paper stated. I wondered why—not why the man died, but why the paper mentioned it, and since it did see fit to do so why it didn't likewise mention that a man ate his breakfast in New York yesterday morning, or that the sun set in London the other night, or any other likely fact. If Philadelphia wasn't so far away from here, or if this departed man had been a great general or an oil magnate or the owner of a brewery or even a mere poet, I could have understood better why his departure should be recorded—but no, he was just a man named Jonas Brown who died suddenly at his home in Philadelphia.

Maybe 'twas the idea of suddenness the paper wished to call attention to as a sort of a warning to us, a reminder that you or I or anybody, either in this city or in Philadelphia, or in London, are liable to pass suddenly away if we don't watch out.

There's only one newspaper I ever really enjoyed. It is yellow and old, and the news in it has been stale these sixty years.

Always just at the study hour, when my brother and I were settling down to our books I felt called upon to bring forth this paper. I simply couldn't endure to see that dear, humorous, don't give a darn, expression on Ted's face give way to one of serious contemplation.

I would read in a solemn voice:
"*New York Evening Post, Saturday, Jan. 27, 1840.*"

My brother would grin with relief, shove his algebra to one side and prepare to listen.

I read, while Ted interrupted with comment and exclamation as follows:

"The second course of lectures before the Mercantile Society has already commenced. Mr. Longfellow, the poet, will deliver two lectures on the life and writings of Dante; and one on the writings of John Paul Richter, one of the most remarkable and eccentric of the German authors.

"Professor Torrey, whose diligence in the pursuit of natural sciences has been rewarded with deserved reputation, will give a course of ten lectures on the chemistry of nature.

"Two lectures on the battle of Chippewa and other engagements on our northwestern frontier during the late war, will be delivered by Professor Douglass, who was present in them.

"R. W. Emerson, an impressive speaker, possessing a peculiar style and mode of thinking, will lecture on the Philosophy of History.

"Professor Longfellow lectures this evening on the life and writings of Dante, at Clinton Hall. If his speculations on this subject be as interesting as his Psalm of Life, it will be well worth attending."

"Sis, we must go to *that*," Ted interrupted. "That Longfellow is a pretty smart fellow. It isn't every one who could write a Psalm." And he repeats with a dreamy look in his eye:

> "Tell me not in mournful numbers
> Life was made fer you 'n me;
> Rudyard Kip has run a corner
> On the things I'd like to be.

> Lives of great Profs. all remind us
>   We can make our lives so pat,
> And departing leave behind us
>   Fossil prints of where we sat."

I silence him. "Listen," I say, "Maggie Beeswax is dead.

Ted hops from his chair. "No, impossible! What, my little Maggie gone? When, oh when did this direful thing occur? Last evening! Even while I slept. But where, Sis, where?"

"At her home in Philadelphia," I read. This is the climax. As I glance at the agonized look on my brother's face I am forced to stuff my handkerchief down my throat, for gravity is essential to the spirit of such a play.

Poor little Maggie Beeswax! If you only had had some other name we never should have been so irreverent.

I proceed. "Married. On the twenty-first inst. by the Rev. H. Chase, Mr. Benj. B. Henrich, to Miss Angelina J., daughter of Orick Fisher, Esq., of this city."

I hear Ted crying out, "Oh, my little Angelina J. how could you be so perfidious! I thought you were all mine own, but alas, you are hisn! How am I to bear my pain? Sis," he adds, "*don't* tell me she was married in Phila.—*don't* do it!"

Then follows a very sarcastic cutting paragraph written by a certain John Smith who claimed to be related to the John Smith who cut off Pocahontas' head—no, she cut off his head or else she *didn't* cut it off, anyhow there was a head mixed up in it somewhere.

This John Smith said a great many cutting bitter things about Henry Clay's speech that was delivered in the Senate day before yesterday, Jan. 25, 1840.

It made Ted horrible mad at Smith and he paced the floor in anger. "Do you think I'll have my old chum, Henry, abused in that manner? Why, Henry and I were schoolmates, and I remember well the day he spoke 'Twinkle, twinkle little star.'"

"On Friday eve," I proceed, "the Rev. and Honorable Henry Clay delivered an oration over the body of Judge White. Deacon Daniel Webster, the great constitutional humbug, was not present. It is said that he was invited to attend, but that, whilst sojourning in England with his 'dear Duke of Rutland,' he actually forgot that such a being as Judge White existed. It is also said that he has scarcely any recollection of such a man as one Henry Clay. Yours, etc."

This made *me* mad. The idea of calling Webster a "great constitutional humbug!"

Ted and I discussed that paragraph at length, sandwiching in many little anecdotes of these great men who had been our schoolmates years before.

"Nonsense!" you say? Of course! And blessed be nonsense! It kept our home in a hubbub of fun, it kept my mother from "blues" and my brother from algebra and *me* from ever going to Vassar and graduating with highest honors out of a class of one hundred and seventy-five. Blessed be Nonsense!

THE END.

www.ingramcontent.com/pod-product-compliance
Lightning Source LLC
Chambersburg PA
CBHW022128160426
43197CB00009B/1198